Céline Sciamma

Visionaries: Thinking Through Female Filmmakers
Series Editors Lucy Bolton and Richard Rushton

Title in the series include:

The Cinema of Marguerite Duras: Multisensoriality and Female Subjectivity
Michelle Royer

Ana Kokkinos: An Oeuvre of Outsiders
Kelly McWilliam

Gillian Armstrong: Popular, Sensual & Ethical Cinema
Julia Erhart

Kathleen Collins: The Black Essai Film
Geetha Ramanathan

Habiba Djahnine: Memory Bearer
Sheila Petty

The Cinema of Mia Hansen-Løve: Candour and Vulnerability
Kate Ince

edinburghuniversitypress.com/series/vision

Céline Sciamma

Portraits

Emma Wilson

EDINBURGH
University Press

Edinburgh University Press is one of the leading university presses in the UK. We publish academic books and journals in our selected subject areas across the humanities and social sciences, combining cutting-edge scholarship with high editorial and production values to produce academic works of lasting importance. For more information visit our website: edinburghuniversitypress.com

We are committed to making research available to a wide audience and are pleased to be publishing Platinum Open Access editions of the ebooks in this series.

Edinburgh University Press Ltd
The Tun – Holyrood Road
12(2f) Jackson's Entry
Edinburgh EH8 8PJ

Typeset in 12/14 Arno and Myriad by
IDSUK (DataConnection) Ltd, and
printed and bound by CPI Group (UK) Ltd, Croydon, CR0 4YY

A CIP record for this book is available from the British Library

ISBN 978 1 4744 4055 4 (hardback)
ISBN 978 1 4744 4591 7 (webready PDF)
ISBN 978 1 4744 2548 3 (paperback)
ISBN 978 1 4744 2550 6 (epub)

Contents

Figures

Acknowledgements

I am thrilled to be published in the Edinburgh University Press 'Visionaries' series. Huge thanks to Lucy Bolton and Richard Rushton for their inspiration and encouragement. It has been a pleasure to work with all at EUP and I am grateful to Gillian Leslie, Richard Strachan, Fiona Conn and Eliza Wright. I would like to express thanks to Stuart Bell, Alice Blackhurst, Lucy Bolton, Clara Bradbury Rance, Chris Brown, Emma Carleschi, Jasmine Cooper, Robbie Duschinsky, Kitty Grady, Blake Gutt, Fiona Handyside, Nick Hammond, Sue Harris, Nick Harrison, Mary Harrod, Stephanie Hemelryk Donald, Pam Hirsch, Kate Ince, Hannah Kilduff, Ashwiny Kistnareddy, Michael Lawrence, Regina Longo, Karen Lury, Laura McMahon, Isabelle McNeill, Despoina Mantziari, Carol Mavor, So Mayer, Margaret Mertz, Ryan Montgomery, Ros Murray, Sophie Niang, Jules O'Dwyer, Martin O'Shaughnessy, Lili Owen-Rowlands, Hannah Parlett, Lili Pickett-Palmer, J. D. Rhodes, B. Ruby Rich, Richard Rushton, Frances Smith, Jackie Stacey, Ginette Vincendeau, Xinyi Wang, and Sarah Wright. My mum, Jacqueline Wilson, loves Sciamma's films too. This book is for my 'daughter' Simone. Lapin, merci, je t'aime.

I draw on writing from two articles previously published:

Wilson, Emma (2014), '"The sea nymphs tested this miracle": *Water Lilies* (2007) and the origin of coral', in Chris Brown and Pam Hirsch (eds), *The Cinema of the Swimming Pool*, Oxford, Bern, Berlin, Brussels, Frankfurt am Main, New York, and Vienna: Peter Lang, pp. 203–14.

Wilson, Emma (2017), 'Scenes of hurt and rapture: Céline Sciamma's *Girlhood*', *Film Quarterly* 70.3: 10–22.

I am grateful for permission to reuse material here. Thanks to Chris Brown and Pam Hirsch for first inviting me to write about Céline Sciamma. Thanks to B. Ruby Rich for being *the* superlative editor.

Introduction: portraits

Sciamma

The filming of Céline Sciamma's fourth film *Portrait de la jeune fille en feu* [*Portrait of a Lady on Fire*] (2019) began with portraits of the director herself. Her cinematographer, Claire Mathon, took analogue photos on the set, starting with images of Sciamma. Mathon describes this as 'a way of questioning differently the relation in creativity between the one who looks and the one who is looked at' (Mathon 2019: n.p.).[1] The artist acted as model at the project's inception.[2] This volume is a study of Sciamma after the success of her fourth film, *Portrait of a Lady on Fire*, which tells the story of a female artist falling in love with the young woman she paints. This manifesto film, a beautiful film about art, and about feminism, offers an optic through which to look back on Sciamma's career to date.

Céline Sciamma is the most visible and important feminist, and lesbian, director in international filmmaking at this moment.[3] She stood next to veteran director Agnès Varda on the steps of the Palais at the Cannes Film Festival in 2018, campaigning for gender parity in the film industry. Sciamma's fourth feature, *Portrait of a Lady on Fire*, competed for the Palme d'Or at Cannes in 2019, and intervened directly in debates about the female gaze, sexuality, and specifically how to look at, and make a portrait of, young women. This feminist intervention has been extended beyond the film through her support for her former partner, actress Adèle Haenel, whose speaking up about sexual abuse has been critical in 2019 and 2020 in France's ongoing reckoning with patriarchal violence and abuse in the film industry, and in society at large.

Sciamma is a director who has made children and adolescents, their vulnerable position in the family, and their autonomy and sensuality, central to her filmmaking. In her approach to female, non-binary, and queer identities she has focused in particular on the need for agency of children and adolescents, binding this imperative into her aesthetic choices and modes of filmmaking. She has been particularly attentive to issues of power and domination, showing how heteronormative families, and larger society, extend control and require submission and consent. She is extremely sensitive to the emotions, to ambivalence and conflicted affect, allowing intensity of feeling to be conveyed even in the sparest narratives. This recognition of complex investments, of confusion, hurt, and tenderness, combined with a clear political agenda, makes her work feel excoriating, energising, and true.

Céline Sciamma was born in 1978, and spent her childhood in Cergy-Pontoise, a 'new' town in the Paris suburbs, filmed by Eric Rohmer in *L'Ami de mon amie* [*My Girlfriend's Boyfriend*] (1987).[4] After studying literature at Paris-Nanterre (one of the French universities centrally involved in May 68) she entered the prestigious film school La Fémis and studied from 2001 to 2005, majoring in screenwriting.[5] The script for her first film, *Naissance des pieuvres* [*Water Lilies*] (2007) was her graduation project. She wrote it with no intention of going on to direct the script. The film was shot in Cergy-Pontoise in 2006 and went on to be selected for the section Un Certain Regard in Cannes in 2007. It also won the Louis Delluc award for a first film. Her second film, *Tomboy* (2011), premiered at the Berlin Film Festival in the Panorama section and won the Teddy award (for films with queer topics). Her third film, *Bande de filles* [*Girlhood*] (2014), screened in the Quinzaine des Réalisateurs section at Cannes. Her fourth, *Portrait of a Lady on Fire*, competed in the Official Selection at Cannes, winning the Best Screenplay Award, and the Queer Palm.

In addition to her *auteure* films, Sciamma has continued to write for other directors, collaborating with André Téchiné on the script for *Quand on a 17 ans* [*Being 17*] (2016),[6] and adapting a novel by Gilles Paris for the stop-motion animated film *Ma Vie de Courgette* [*My Life as a Courgette*] (Claude Barras, 2016). Both of these projects show her interest in childhood and adolescence in the context of broken families, looking at bereavement and adoption, and at fragile links and attachments formed outside family structures. She has recently worked on a script with Jacques Audiard for the film *Les Olympiades* (2021) based on New Yorker cartoonist Adrian Tomine's collection of graphic short stories *Killing and Dying*. She also worked for a year and a half on the TV series *Les Revenants* [*The Returned*] (2012), and several times in interview she expresses the wish to work as director in serial TV. Indeed, this is anticipated in *Girlhood*, which is structured in five 'episodes' with interleaving cuts to darkness.[7]

A marked aspect of Sciamma's films has been their politically charged relation to the moment they are made in, and also to the futures they anticipate. They also have a life of their own, sometimes shifting in meaning in the context in which they are received. Her second film *Tomboy* is about a child (played by Zoé Héran) who, on moving to a new housing estate, is (mis)recognised as a boy by another child, Lisa (Jeanne Disson). Following *Water Lilies*, a girl's lesbian coming-of-age drama, it was initially possible, led in part by director interviews, to read *Tomboy* as a drama of childhood queerness, of a girl whose nascent same-sex desire compels her to identify as a boy. In the decade since the film was released, increasing trans visibility and activism has made it clear that more is at stake. The act of recognition allows the child to assume for the wilderness time of the summer holidays the boy self he is, while continuing to play the roles of girl, daughter, and sister in his family. Even if it was not intended as such, *Tomboy* is precious as an index of the sensory reality of a trans boy, and this, it appears, is one of the stories it tells.

Time has also already brought changing perspectives on Sciamma's third film, *Girlhood*, a film about a girl Marieme

(Karidja Touré) in the Parisian *banlieue* leaving school, after being denied access to the academic stream of education and joining a gang. The film is made with a cast that is majority Black and was initially received as a new feminist vision of the *banlieue* twenty years on from *La Haine* (Mathieu Kassovitz, 1995). There were ambivalences about the film already on its release. The important moves in the decolonise movement and in particular the visibility of Black Lives Matter in Europe as well as the US in the years immediately subsequent to the making of the film have made it increasingly hard to appreciate a film made by a white director, and predominantly white crew, about Black lives in France. Political activism and a shifting climate have revealed oversights in the film. However beautiful the film is visually and accomplished as a narrative, and however committed it is to visibility of young women of colour – both the characters and the actresses – on screen, it needs now to be viewed with awareness of the criticisms it has generated from Black scholars.

A different shift, and movement in time, is witnessed in the even shorter afterlife of Sciamma's most recent film, *Portrait of a Lady on Fire*. In its selection to compete in Cannes, and alliances visually with the work of Jane Campion, whose film *The Piano* (1993) is the only film to date by a woman to win the Palme d'Or, *Portrait of a Lady on Fire* offered visibility to women directors in the film industry.[8] Sciamma is a founding signatory of the movement 50/50 by 2020, an equality initiative launched in 2018 to work towards gender parity in the French film industry.[9] Her film gained more relevance to contemporary feminism through its lead actress Adèle Haenel's decision in 2019 to speak out about the abuse and harassment she received as a child by director Christophe Ruggia. Her courage in facing this, and Sciamma's support for her, allowed issues about patriarchy, the film industry, and tolerance for abuse to be made visible. This was a critical moment in French response to #metoo and in shifting opinions. *Portrait of a Lady on Fire*, with what Alice Blackhurst describes as 'a sexual dynamic not dependent on predation, domination, or imbalances of power' (2019: n.p.), was powerfully available as a counter example. It was rightly adored by a young, female, feminist audience.[10]

Sciamma's films metamorphose. I look at them as living things existing in time, rousing sometimes contrary, complex feelings. Metamorphosis is also one of their subjects, as they show young protagonists awakening and changing. Thomas Sotinel, reviewing *Portrait of a Lady on Fire*, writes of her films, 'the flourishing of their characters resembles a metamorphosis' (2019: 25).[11] For Jonathan Romney, writing about a different film, and reading metamorphosis as perpetual, '[t]he young heroines of *Girlhood* are perplexing shape-shifters' (2015: n.p.). Metamorphosis relates to adolescence, but its treatment by Sciamma belies a commitment to unfixing, of identity, and even of meaning, where she commits to what is mercurial and transient.[12] She herself comments on the strange experience of change as she was filming *Water Lilies*: 'it was a very emotional thing filming Pauline Acquart [who plays Marie]: her body was changing over the time of the shoot' (Garbarz and Martinez 2014: 27).[13] Her filming meets her changing subjects.

As if to link contemporary coming-of-age stories to a far longer history of transitions, *Portrait of a Lady on Fire* refers explicitly to the classical text, Ovid's *Metamorphoses*, with its multiple stories of changes of body, gender, form, and matter. The tale that is referenced directly in the film is that of Orpheus and Eurydice, where the poet and lover Orpheus attempts to retrieve his dead beloved from the Underworld. But other tales in Ovid illuminate Sciamma's themes, the tale of sea nymphs and the birth of coral, and the story of Tiresias who was transformed into a woman and was able to compare male and female pleasure. Bodies as impressionable, and ever changing, are her subject. She has said, indeed, that she would be interested in making a fantasy film in order to work on the strangeness of bodies growing and mutating (Garbarz and Martinez 2014: 27). She draws from Ovid an interest in matter and substance, and specifically their mutability. Recalling Ovid in thinking about Sciamma reveals the ways in which her work, although strikingly original, is always in dialogue with a wider range of literary and artistic reference. Although its subject matter, up until *Portrait of a Lady on Fire*, is very contemporary, her themes are also immemorial.

In thinking about Sciamma and the contemporary moment, I am inspired by recent French writing on feminism, in order to understand the immediate political and theoretical context of her filmmaking in France. Beyond this, and taking a longer view, I turn to the history of art, to feminist engagements with the visual, and to films, photographs, paintings, and sculptures by women artists who share concerns with Sciamma. In an industry such as cinema, so entrenched in patriarchal relations, painting and photography, and also myth and literature, offer new inspiration. Sciamma's work is vitally cinematic, and reflective about cinema as art form, and about French cinema in particular, but like a portrait painter, or a novelist, she also attends passionately to her subjects, to their apprehensions, their attachments, and their being in the world.

Domination

In 2018 Manon Garcia published *On ne naît pas soumise, on le devient* [*One is not born submissive, one becomes it*] (2018) written in response to the #metoo movement in the US and France, and offering a new acclamation of the importance of the work of Simone de Beauvoir for contemporary feminism.[14] I see it as a strong point of reference for thinking about Sciamma's films. This comes in particular in its focus on identity as embodied and its attention to the importance of childhood and changes in puberty as they inter-relate with the social construction of binary identity, and the difference of being a girl. Young women's need for self-possession, and the threat to this from the objectification of their bodies under patriarchy, comes strongly to light in Garcia's work, following Beauvoir. The question of the self-possession and agency of children and young women is an enduring concern in Sciamma's films, from her coming-of-age projects to her reflections on looking, power, and equality in *Portrait of a Lady on Fire*.

Psychoanalyst Geneviève Morel begins an article on *Tomboy*: 'To parody a famous statement by Simone de Beauvoir: how does one become a girl in the 21st century?' (2012: 65).[15] Garcia adapts Beauvoir's adage that one is not born a woman but becomes one, to think particularly about women's submission to men, and women's subjugation within a larger patriarchal system. For Garcia, it is important to think in more detail about what women submit to, and what that experience of submission is, both psychically and in embodied terms. She argues that 'as women, they undergo a form of domination which is in part social but which is manifested above all in interpersonal relations' (2018: 108).[16] Women's experience of submission is structural, prescribed by the structure of society which is still far from egalitarian (2018: 109). And it is also one-to-one, interpersonal relations repeating the larger structure of domination learnt and prescribed in society at large. Garcia sees the inter-relation between interpersonal instances of subjugation, such as sexual harassment, violence against women, and femicide – all the focus of #metoo and contemporary feminism in France – and a wider social structure. The intersection of difference in relation to class, race, and other markers of difference is critical here, but for Garcia all women live this structural submission in patriarchy. What is critical in Garcia and Beauvoir for Sciamma is their emphasis on girlhood.

Following Beauvoir, Garcia identifies the importance of childhood and adolescence in the apprehension of submission. Puberty marks the moment when the young girl comes to see her body as an object that is looked at by others, suddenly understanding that her body is sexualised by the male gaze (2018: 184). For Garcia, 'her body has become something that no longer belongs to her, which is no longer her body, but a woman's body, namely an object of desire for the male gaze' (2018: 185).[17] It is the understanding of this moment and its meaning that is critical to contemporary French feminism, and to its undoing the subjugation that this sense of being looked at, desired, implies. Garcia speaks about puberty as a time of transition, that also involves a reckoning with the objectification of the body (2018: 184). There is something alienating in this time of metamorphosis being also one of dispossession. Garcia lays moving emphasis on the child's 'gêne', the French term signalling 'trouble', 'embarrass-ment', and also 'distress' (2018: 140). The girl's body no longer seems to belong to her. It exists for men instead, in their gaze (2018: 187), and she is divided from her own body and feelings.

The focus on childhood and adolescence in Sciamma's first three films can be seen in a political light in this context. Sciamma is interested in showing and making visible the ways in which children and adolescents are subjugated by the laws of patriarchy and binary gender.[18] She is also concerned with finding different, less alienating ways of looking and being in her films. Beauvoir, and Garcia following her, have drawn attention to the young girl's body as central to this first realisation of objectification and alienation. Sciamma shows the 'gêne', the distress, of young girls, and takes it seriously. The attention to sensory detail, embodied realities, also in this sense has a political edge. She identifies alienation. Rather than looking away from the body, she imagines different ways of taking pleasure in it. Her work is sensually rich, as well as politically cogent. In her coming-of-age dramas, in her attention to child and adolescent bodies, she imagines different outcomes that do not prescribe submission. If they do show subjugation at certain moments – to the law of binary gender in *Tomboy*, for example – they make visible the pain of that submission. In her fourth film, she envisages the possibility of thinking about looking, and erotic apprehension of the body, outside structures of domination. This work she pursues with her former partner, whose own life experiences lend urgency and authenticity to the issues at hand.

The alienation of the young girl described by Garcia has disturbing resonances with the extreme experiences of Adèle Haenel in her encounter with Christophe Ruggia.[19] In interviews Haenel draws attention to her feelings of guilt and powerlessness, and to the particular violence of keeping silent, of feeling gagged and unable to speak. She makes clear that this silencing was not chosen but undergone, and she sees her choice to speak out as an act of solidarity with other victims of abuse.[20] Garcia's work on submission and subjugation allows the continuities between becoming a woman, and being looked at and objectified under patriarchy, and being subjected to abuse and violence, to come to light. Sciamma's work does not draw directly from Haenel's experience, but exists as an artistic reflection on, and vision of, survival beyond the girlhood narratives that Haenel and others are making public.

Sciamma's work also moves beyond Garcia to consider non-binary identities, that of a trans boy, as well as those of girls and young women. For Sciamma's critique of patriarchy, and her embrace of non-binary identities, the work of Paul B. Preciado is revelatory and in line with Garcia.[21] In *Je suis un monstre qui vous parle* [*I am a monster who is talking to you*] (2020b), Preciado also thinks about patriarchy and subjugation, arguing that a feminist and queer rereading of the Oedipus complex according to Freud is urgently needed.[22] Showing the ways in which psychoanalysis has failed to listen to, and account for, queer desires and non-binary being in the world, he specifically critiques the reading of incestuous desire in Freud, which is, for Preciado, a patriarchal crime:

> I can say, very quickly, that by placing the blame on Oedipus and in putting the weight of analysis on his supposed 'incestuous desire', Freud and psychoanalysis have contributed to the stability of male domination, making the victim responsible for rape and making the social rituals of normalisation of gender, sexual violence and abuse of children and women which are the basis of patriarcho-colonial culture into psychic laws. (Preciado 2020b: 83–4)[23]

In the contemporary moment, where abuse is being called out, psychoanalysts can no longer talk about the Oedipus complex or the Name of the Father.[24] Preciado, like Garcia, sees a line between male domination in patriarchy, binary gender, and sexual predation. He envisages childhood as the time of subjugation under these laws, writing of his own transition:

> It's more than six years since I abandoned the juridical and political status of woman. A time that seems short when considered from the deafening comfort of normative identity, but infinitely long when everything that has been learnt in childhood has to be unlearnt. (Preciado 2020b: 20)[25]

Preciado identifies psychoanalysis with the social system which is produced by, and produces, male domination. He looks for a freeing of children and adolescents from predation and abuse, and also from the structures which facilitate male domination and binary gender.

Like Preciado, Sciamma sees the subjugation of women and children in a broader frame that includes gender non-conforming people. She sees puberty and adolescence as critical to understanding and contesting patriarchy, and bound up in this is a rejection of the body as an object sexualised by others. Sciamma advocates child and adolescent agency, autonomy, and self-possession. She looks towards choice, consent, and freedom. She offers ways of thinking about, and looking at, the body that move away from the categories and power relations of binary gender.

Sciamma thinks beyond the phallus and castration, valuing different body morphologies, and opening polymorphous pleasures. This is how she too, like Preciado, is moving towards a new history of sexuality. She creates moments in film that speak of lesbian and non-binary experience.[26] She lets these moments take on the aura of romance, a cinematic enchantment, a string of lights around the heart. She points to the way their existence in film, in France and globally, is politically important. If she is a director who has focused in on distress, embarrassment, and hurt, she is also interested in new moments of joy and pleasure.

As I look at her films, I am interested in the ways in which she mobilises moving image art as a means to achieve these goals. Showing children, girls, and young women, as mobile, and transforming, is key to this. Sciamma's filmmaking seeks to rethink the visual, beauty, and pleasure. This is how she looks for a means of refusing objectification and so ending a regime of domination.[27]

Inclinations

Sciamma's critique of patriarchy and subjugation requires new ways of using the moving image medium and reflection on how bodies are shown on screen. Feminist philosophy and the history of art help identify the means she uses. For example, in her 2016 volume *Inclinations*, Adriana Cavarero offers an argument for thinking a relational ontology marked by a feminist critique of (patriarchal ideas of) uprightness and rectitude. She replaces rectitude with inclining, remarking that 'to incline is to bend, to lean down, to lower' (2016: 3). 'Inclination bends and dispossesses the I' (2016: 7), she says. She envisages 'a kind of subjectivity already caught up in folds, dependencies, exposures, dramas, knots, and bonds' (2016: 130).[28] Cavarero's turn to think these issues through painting, pose, and gesture allows thought about the interest of her work, between philosophy and history of art, for feminist film, and specifically for the work of Sciamma.

The kind of subjectivity involved in inclining is, for Cavarero, the maternal. Developing a *postural* ethics she highlights 'maternal inclination – understood as a posture that is relational, originary, and asymmetrical, capable of evoking a common vulnerability' (2016: 127).[29] Her sense that a pose carries some vision of relation and intersubjectivity is compelling, and holds potential for thinking about how, and in what positions, the body is shown on screen. But Cavarero in *Inclinations* remains within the normative family structure in thinking the mother's inclination to the child. (Her work in *Relating Narratives* (2000) opens to different structures in thinking female friendship.)

Sciamma too looks for a different relational ontology rooted in a different way of positioning and imaging faces and bodies, and she moves outside the mother and child relation. One alternative part of Sciamma's feminism, and its visual, pictorial realisation, is found in the postures through which she illustrates dramas, knots and bonds between children, women, and non-binary people, who are siblings, friends, and lovers. This is part of her thinking of the body beyond domination. She privileges agency and autonomy, but also, like Cavarero, shows how subjects exist exposed and in inter-relation, never fully knowing or understanding themselves or the others they love.

Cavarero looks to Renaissance art to find a different model for thinking ethical and feminist relationality. In looking to illuminate Sciamma's film frames and the feelings they hold, I make comparisons with modern and contemporary works, paintings from the eighteenth century forwards, sculptures, and photographs, by women artists. This is to recognise the involvement of Sciamma's work aesthetically with feminist work in other mediums, so illuminating her visual and spatial choices. This is not to trace influences but to find connections between different imagining and framing of bodies in feminist art. It is also a strategy to make visible some other artists who have in different ways kinship with Sciamma and shared ethos. In this aim to look at her works alongside those of other artists I am inspired by the work of two feminist art historians, Griselda Pollock and Carol Mavor.

In conjuring the idea of a 'virtual feminist museum', in her book project of 2007, Pollock imagines new ways of curating art and new encounters with artworks by women. She draws attention to possibilities for a feminist remapping of the museum space and newly politicised understandings of the exposure of the body in art. The virtual feminist museum, drawing on and rethinking the work of Aby Warburg in his Mnemosyne project, becomes a space for expression of new relations and for forms of activism.

More recently, looking at works by Sonia Khurana and Sutapa Biswas, Pollock writes: 'One key focus of the Virtual Feminist Museum concerns the ethics and body politics of one specific "pathos formula": lying down' (2018: n.p.).[30] Like Cavarero looking at inclination, Pollock is interested in a pose and gesture, for her, reclining or lying prone. She thinks about the politically charged adoption of lying down in contemporary works. Khurana's performance *Lying-down-on-the-ground* (2006–12), in Pollock's reading, draws out intense emotions:

> Lying down 'speaks' the weight of the trauma of psychological dereliction in the pathos of that act of giving way, desiring the support of bare earth or hard ground, or giving into a wish to escape into unconsciousness or sleep that might also feel like death. (Pollock 2018: n.p.)

For Pollock, the story and pose of Sleeping Beauty 'represents the imposed passivity of women in patriarchal culture' (2018: n.p.). She finds in the work of the artists she examines a different energy and aim. She writes: 'Sometimes we place our bodies nakedly and vulnerably in the world of history or in the landscapes of memory' (2018: n.p.). Pollock draws attention to possible reactivating and transforming of meanings, in repeating and shifting poses and gestures, moves and shapes.

In her different feminist art historical practice, Mavor gathers images with startling emotive, sensory, and formal connections, in a Proustian way letting links be apprehended by intuition, by sudden shock, by involuntary memory. Mavor juxtaposes words and images in her projects, telling stories and letting a dissolving sweep of images mesmerise the viewer. For Mavor, artworks, the field of the visual, hold sometimes unspeakable, intense, and bruising feelings, grief, an erotic charge, regression, joy. She is attentive to colour, texture, surface, the transparent, the glassy, the diaphanous. Her range of images, visual and verbal, by women artists, runs from Julia Margaret Cameron's sensual images, dreamy, 'otherworldly', of children, to Toni Morrison's *The Bluest Eye* (1970), Carrie Mae Weems's *Blue Black Boy* (1997), and Colette conjuring a memory of a field of blue wildflowers she saw as a girl. Mavor's work, like Sciamma's, is attentive to the sensorium of children, and connects this, through art, to adult consciousness.

As a filmmaker Sciamma has recourse to movement and changing angles of vision in her artworks. As a feminist, post

Beauvoir, she is sensitive to the body as part of our situation and being in the world. She is interested in the selfhood exposed, and hidden, in bodily pose and gesture, as well as facial expression. Looking at her films with Pollock lets her films be read as new iterations or reactivations of poses in art. And her portraits are also about feeling, about relaying emotions, if of the body then also of the psyche. Sciamma creates sensory worlds in her films, that are not only formally controlled but expressive, beyond language, particularly of the rarefied feelings of childhood and adolescence. Their affective charge is illuminated by Mavor.

Sciamma draws attention to the vulnerability and plasticity of young bodies. Her intelligent focus on her protagonists, and sparse, finely judged writing, lead her to conceive human, complex, sensitively drawn, and very real characters. Her portraits in film attend to the moves and needs of their subjects, without claiming to catch an essence, a true self. The films look at embodied existence, sensory life, gestures, emotions, silence, and stillness. Sciamma offers multiple, serial images. Her subjects are never fixed.

Portrait of a Young Girl in Brussels

Painting and photography are important in this study, but Sciamma's portraits of young girls can also be compared with works by a host of film directors, for example Jane Campion's *A Girl's Own Story* (1986),[31] Catherine Breillat's *Une Vraie Jeune Fille* [*A Real Young Girl*] (1976), Julia Ducournau's *Grave* [*Raw*] (2016), Rebecca Zlotowski's *Une Fille facile* [*An Easy Girl*] (2019), or the various girl-led dramas of Mia Hansen-Løve or Alice Rohrwacher. Sciamma herself speaks of her encounter with 'le jeune cinéma français' in the 1990s and the influence of Noémie Lvovsky's film about four girls, *La Vie ne me fait pas peur* [*Life Doesn't Scare Me*] (1999). Over and above these connections, the one film which offers the closest anticipation of Sciamma's work, and pre-empts its poignancy and truth about childhood and adolescence, is Chantal Akerman's *Portrait d'une jeune fille de la fin des années 60 à Bruxelles* [*Portrait of a Young Girl in the Late 60s in Brussels*] (1994), an hour-long film made for ARTE.[32] The very title of Akerman's film is echoed, perhaps unintentionally, in Sciamma's recent title *Portrait of a Lady on Fire*.[33]

At the centre of Akerman's film is a party sequence. Michelle (Circe Lethem), in a striped shirt stands out from the other girls. Her mood is melancholy. A song, 'La Bamba', plays at the party. Danielle (Joelle Marlier), in a peppermint green dress, invites Michelle into the centre of the ring. For beautiful moments, Michelle and Danielle face each other dancing together. The music and ring of faces creates a blurred, vibrant ground for this unreal happening. Danielle has chosen Michelle. She takes her by the hand. Michelle glows with happiness. She is entranced by Danielle, by her prettiness. This is a *coup de foudre*, an interpolation. Danielle invites Michelle. She catches her in desire. Then Danielle goes back into the circle. She is glimpsed from behind, her dark hair hanging down. She finds her place, with a boy beside her. Michelle is alone.

The song continues, its sounds heightened. Michelle does not exit. She is as if arrested. She is alone, moving but unable to move on. She watches the dancers circle, and then chooses Danielle again. There is a hiatus in Michelle's sense of self. She is suddenly exposed, lost. The film is painful in capturing her faltering. Danielle joins her. The repetition, the return to the ring, undoes the ritual. Akerman's choice to have them do this again is devastating, about madness and impossibility. Michelle looks at Danielle, and Danielle's shadow falls across her.

The music shifts to 'It's a Man's World'. A boy cuts in and takes Danielle in his arms. Michelle is again on her own. Her face is close to the camera and the camera stays with her as she stays numb. She watches and there is no cut-away. Her lack of join with the world is felt. She stands, in readiness. There is pathos in the camera's attention to her, her face impassive as she waits. And then she turns and leaves. She goes into the dark garden outside, passing a boy who wears her same striped shirt. She paces alone on the green lawn. The moment of love is lost. But it was present in the dance, with manic joy.

Flashforward a decade or two to Sciamma's films. There is the first love of *Water Lilies* with its parties and dancing. There is the interpolation of Mickäel in *Tomboy* where, with Lisa, he can exist, miraculously, as a boy. Like Akerman, Sciamma is a director who needs very few words to conjure feeling. Sciamma's directing of actors, her understanding of gesture and mood, are enough to allow the moving images to hold pathos and meaning. Akerman shows multiple shifting images of Michelle in her striped shirt, her dark hair tied back, and Sciamma likewise returns to the girls she films, showing them always different, catching minute shifts in response, thought, and feeling. Sciamma follows Akerman in her attention to the intensity, grief, and elation of growing up. Sciamma moves forwards with these emotions. If for Akerman this is about existence, opening to the world, Sciamma is more focused on a clear, and liberatory, political agenda.

Scopophilia

Sciamma is an imaginative portraitist. This is felt in her attention to the range of feelings, and to the becoming, the destinies, of her young protagonists. It is achieved in her extraordinary participatory and collaborative work with young actors. Children and young women are dwelt on, photographed in her filmmaking but, through Sciamma's creative uses of her medium, never fixed, always moving and moving on. This approach to portraiture is witnessed in her creation of still and barely moving, shifting, serial, frontal images of her protagonists, of the child in *Tomboy*, drawn by his sister, of Adèle Haenel as a young woman, Héloïse, in *Portrait of a Lady on Fire*.

Where Sciamma may be compared to women photographers who have explored seriality and changes over time, such as Rineke Dijkstra, and who have pursued narrative sequences of images, such as Carrie Mae Weems (as discussed in my chapter on *Girlhood*), the photographer who has come closest, for me, to illuminating the lives of female and non-binary children and young people, and making portraits of them, in ways revelatory for Sciamma, is Nan Goldin, the New York-, Berlin-, and Paris-based American photographer.

Goldin's 2014 volume *Eden and After*, created with Guido Costa, gathers together photographs of children from throughout Goldin's career. In interview with Ella Alexander in *Vogue*, published on the book's appearance, Goldin says, recalling Garcia and Preciado:

> With children, society starts destroying them quickly, but before they're four or five they have their own worlds. I have this idea that children come from another planet; they remember that place at first then they forget it. This book shows children as autonomous beings; it's not about children as invented by adults, not about behaving in ways that were prescribed to them. (Alexander 2014: n.p.)

Speaking in an essay in the same volume, of what he sees as Nan's unique empathy with children, Costa names them 'creatures who in their unwillingness to yield are doomed to suffer a gradual, inevitable subjugation' (Goldin 2014: 376). Like Goldin, Sciamma envisages children as autonomous, as living in their own worlds that, through her careful work with actors, and her lively imagination, she is able to create on screen.

Both Goldin and Sciamma frequently show children without adults present. In their portraits, photographic and filmic, they attend to the real spaces children live in and fashion, and also to their play and imagination. This is about taking children seriously as subjects, adapting their mediums to make portraits of children on their own terms. These children are not seen as miniature adults, or as objects for idealisation and cherishing. From *Courgette*, the stop-motion puppet, to Mickäel's small *femme* sister Jeanne (Malonn Lévana), Sciamma lets her children be real, impressionable subjects. If Goldin opens an alternative paradise where children run free and wild, self-motivated, creative, beautiful, Sciamma in her portraits of children is interested in the 'inevitable subjugation' that children undergo, and uses her films to detail this, and also to decry it. An area of sensitivity in Sciamma's work is its questioning of compulsory heterosexuality and binary gender, each of the films in its own way using portraiture, close-up attention to children and adolescents alone, and in intimate contact, to chart the ways in which physical and affective lives and intensities outreach these laws. This is in parallel with two sections in *Eden and After*: 'I'm a little girl, I'm a little boy' (2014: 110–31) and 'Girl love' (2014: 164–87).

In 'I'm a little girl, I'm a little boy', the kids flout gender norms. In *Io in camouflage, NYC* (1994), Io in army gear, face painted khaki and green, looks out at the camera. In other photos, the same child holds out a plastic mermaid, lies reading *The Hardy Boys*, and climbs on a wolf statue in Central Park. In another photo, Lucien, hair long, is among the arcades in Coney Island. In others, Tara is in a leather jacket on a bike, and Elio is in a feather boa in the back of a car. These kids are gender queer, fluid, changing.

In 'Girl love', Goldin closes in on the intimacy of girl friendships. *Mia washing Georgia in the tub, London* (2007) is followed by several further pictures of these same little girls in the bath. *Luna and Emma napping, Helsinki* (2010) shows two different little girls in bed, with their own intimacy and connection. Goldin can conjure the force and dignity of these childhood attachments and their sensory worlds. She takes seriously children's lived, chosen, real, and imagined identities, their individuality and sociality at once. She shows children as not always straight and not always binary, but without fixing and labelling, by just observing and feeling.

Both Goldin and Sciamma explore how visual mediums can offer sensuous, visually gorgeous, but liberating, non-voyeuristic ways of looking at faces and bodies. More directly than Sciamma, Goldin has claimed scopophilia, pleasure in looking, as part of her project as a photographer, this name being given to an ongoing series of works which began in 2010 with a commission to work with Patrice Chéreau in the Louvre Museum. Goldin spent time in the museum photographing and responding to a vast range of paintings, largely portraits and nudes. She created a slideshow, *Scopophilia*, which played with transitions between her photographs from the museum and her own images of lovers and friends from her retrospective career. Such comparisons, and resemblances, she explored further in a series of grid pictures and portraits where a loved one and a painting are aligned.

One such alignment (seen in Goldin 2016: 192–3) shows Guérin's *Portrait of a Young Girl* (1812) as photographed by Goldin the Louvre in 2010, next to her photograph *Siobhan, Berlin* (1993). Guérin's painting shows the face and torso of a naked girl. Her short hair is tousled. She is grave and intent, her skin like pearl. She has a mix of androgyny and unmarked femininity. This girl is juxtaposed with Siobhan, her torso naked but Calvin Klein underwear visible. Her stature and affect are more confrontational, more reflective. She looks out of the portrait with a loosely made bed behind her. She was Goldin's lover for five years. In *Nan Goldin, In My Life* (Paul Tschinkel, 1997), Goldin says: 'it was a big part of our relationship for me to photograph her'. In *Scopophilia*, these images of Siobhan's nakedness, mementoes of love, tokens of an earlier time, candid, beautiful portraits, find their way back into Goldin's art.

The contemporary photograph of Siobhan is compared with a Romantic portrait. The two aligned have uncanny resemblances, a similar pose, exposure and reticence, energy and pathos, as each young woman seems strangely alive and also inscrutable. Goldin shows continuities between her own photographs and portraits of young women in the Western tradition in art. She questions the alignment of her pleasure in looking with the scopophilia of Western art. She also queers that tradition, making her portraits of her female lover part of a larger series of stories about the body and looking. Her politics are expansive and inclusive. She embraces historical paintings, showing looking itself as pleasure, as erotic.

Sciamma creates beautiful images in her films, curating sensory environments, worlds of light and colour, as she works closely with cinematographers Crystel Fournier and Claire Mathon. Looking is one of the pleasures of her films, looks in the films, the look of the director at her subjects, the look of the viewer at the films. This is beyond and despite her feminist recognition of the relation between looking, objectification, and subjugation. This is indeed one of the interesting tensions of her projects. Sciamma's work explores ways in which looking may no longer impose a gendered binary of activity and passivity. Looking and being looked at are collaborative, shifting, unfixed. As in Goldin's *Scopophilia*, female beauty, desire in looking, are seen differently, in a fluid, queer domain of pleasure. Sciamma's work, like Goldin's, depends on a certain alchemy, closeness and trust, where the artist's consensual intimacy with her subjects is part of the process of imaging. Sciamma makes art that opens the range of images of children cis and trans, young girls, and women, looking, and looked at, existing in the world.[34] As I write she is working on a new project, *Petite Maman*, which will for sure extend this range, and confirm her unique position still further.

Notes

1 'une manière de questionner autrement le rapport de création entre celui qui regarde et celui qui est regardé'. Translations from the French are mine unless otherwise stated.

2 Sciamma has a cameo, as a server in McDonald's, in her first film.

3 In September 2012 *Cahiers du cinéma* devoted an issue to women filmmakers, since no films by women directors were in competition at Cannes that summer. Céline Sciamma's interview stands out. She argues that women's cinema is an issue not of aesthetics, but of politics. See Sciamma (2012: 25). In the words of So Mayer: 'Céline Sciamma is the most exciting thing to happen to French cinema since Catherine Breillat's *Romance* (1999) definitively blew up *le cinéma du papa*' (2015: n.p.).

4 This is also the town where writer Annie Ernaux lives. Ernaux too has done much to represent class mobility and the lives of women and girls.

5 See Garbarz and Martinez (2014) for further details about Sciamma's studies before film school.

6 This was Téchiné's first film with an original screenplay since *Les Témoins* [*The Witnesses*] (2007). Sciamma has talked about how important Téchiné was to her cinephile formation when she first saw his major films in her teens (Gilson 2016). She has said that Téchiné came to her for two reasons:

the importance of adolescence as a theme in her work and his admiration for the clarity of the narrative line in *Tomboy* (LMC 2016). Sciamma speaks movingly in one interview about her vision of her work with Andre Téchiné, and of the work of a screenwriter in general, which requires being responsive to the filmmaker (*accueillir le cinéaste*) in order to create the best tool to allow their particular filming style to be enhanced (Gilson 2016).

7 This is an inspiration for the structure of this book, where each of the five chapters has five sections.

8 Iris Brey offers a comparison between Sciamma's *Portrait of a Lady on Fire* and Campion's film (2020: 61).

9 In this context she was a co-organiser of the women's march on the red carpet at Cannes later in 2018.

10 I witnessed this on first viewing the film in the 'Cannes à Paris' festival in May 2019.

11 'l'épanouissement de leurs personnages touche à la métamorphose'.

12 Metamorphosis, and the specific emergence of the butterfly from the caterpillar's cocoon, is used more overtly as metaphor in Leonie Krippendorf's queer coming-of-age film *Kokon* [*Cocoon*] (2020).

13 'c'était une grande émotion de filmer Pauline Acquart: son corps évoluait au fil du tournage'.

14 Garcia's book also draws on her French doctoral thesis on submission. Coincidentally, she is the daughter of documentary maker Claire Simon. See Boulé and Tidd (2012) for an important reckoning with Beauvoir as theorist for thinking cinema, and Ince (2017) for a film theoretical reading of Beauvoir as phenomenologist and the implications of this for examining subjectivity in films by female directors.

15 'Pour parodier un célèbre propos de Simone de Beauvoir: comment devient-on fille au XXIe siècle?'

16 'en tant que femmes, elles subissent une forme de domination qui est en partie sociale mais qui se manifeste avant tout dans des rapports interindividuels'.

17 'son corps est devenu quelque chose qui ne lui appartient plus, qui est non plus son corps à elle, mais un corps de femme, c'est-à-dire dans le regard des hommes, un objet de désir'.

18 Véronique Cauhapé writes that Sciamma explores in *Portrait of a Lady on Fire* 'what woman have been submitted to by men's law and how they have managed, sometimes, to get around it' ('ce à quoi les femmes ont été soumises par la loi des hommes et comment elles sont parvenues, parfois, à la contourner') (2019: 18).

19 For a fuller account, see Dryef (2019: 23).

20 In *Le Consentement* [*Consent*] (2020: 131), an account of experience of abusive relations, Vanessa Springora likewise speaks of a nameless

violence. She draws attention to the adaptations an adolescent will make to a situation which she also sees and knows as abnormal and abusive.

21 Haenel participated in Preciado's public and performative seminars at the Centre Pompidou, 'A new history of sexuality' ('Une nouvelle histoire de la sexualité), October 2020.

22 Preciado describes it as the 'Discourse of a trans man, with a non-binary body, before the Freudian School in France' ('Discours d'un homme trans, d'un corps non-binaire, devant l'Ecole de la cause freudienne en France'). The original talk was given in Paris on 17 November 2019. The published version also addresses the responses from the audience. The book is dedicated to Judith Butler. It follows Preciado's work in *Testo Junkie* (2013) and *Un Appartement sur Uranus* (*An Apartment on Uranus*) (2019; 2020 in English) where, in broader theoretical discussion, he speaks of his own departures from binary gender. Catherine Malabou, in discussion of Preciado, speaks of 'the metamorphoses of his body and gender' ('les métamorphoses de son corps et de son genre') (2020: 94).

23 'je peux dire, très rapidement, qu'en portant la faute sur Oedipe et en mettant tout le poids de l'analyse sur son supposé "désir incestueux", Freud et la psychanalyse ont contribué à la stabilité de la domination masculine, en rendant la victime responsable du viol et en transformant en loi psychique les rituels sociaux de normalisation du genre, de violence sexuelle et d'abus des enfants et des femmes qui fonde la culture patriarco-coloniale'.

24 The full quotation runs: 'You can no longer go on talking about the Oedipus Complex or the Name of the Father in a society which is recognising for the first time in history its femicidal functioning, where the victims of patriarchal violence are expressing themselves to denounce their fathers, their husbands, their bosses, their boyfriends; where women are denouncing the institutionalised politics of rape, where thousands of bodies are going into the streets to denounce homophobic attacks and the nearly daily murder of trans women, and the institutionalised forms of racism' ('Vous ne pouvez plus continuer à parler du complexe d'Oedipe ou du nom du père dans une société qui reconnaît pour la première fois dans l'histoire ses fonctionnements féminicides, où les victimes de la violence patriarcale s'expriment pour dénoncer leurs pères, leurs maris, leurs chefs, leurs petits-amis; où les femmes dénoncent la politique institutionalisée du viol, où des milliers de corps descendent dans la rue pour dénoncer les agressions homophobes et les meurtres presque quotidiens des femmes trans, ainsi que les formes institutionalisées du racisme' (Preciado 2020b: 119–20). He responds here to the political issues importantly at the centre of activist protest in France from 2019.

25 'Cela fait plus de six ans que j'ai abandonné le statut juridique et politique de femme. Un temps peut-être court quand on le considère installé dans le confort assourdissant de l'identité normative, mais infiniment long quand tout ce qui a été appris dans l'enfance doit être désappris.'

26 Few such moments have been filmed by women directors in France. (Catherine Corsini's *La Belle Saison* [*Summertime*] (2015) is an exception as a complex love story between women.)

27 After *Portrait of a Lady on Fire* was screened at Cannes, Sciamma was interviewed by Iris Brey for the series of podcasts 'She Cannes' (Sciamma 2019). She speaks about equality being the project of her work, about her awareness of inequalities in the industry, and about her aims to represent love and sex between women in new ways. She sees this as her twelve-year project to date, and one where she is changing and challenging herself. She looks to think beyond submission and power relations, in looking, and in representations of love and sex, seeking other sensations and pleasures.

28 Cavarero has been important for Judith Butler's work in *Giving an Account of Oneself* (2005). Butler has engaged with Cavarero's work *Relating Narratives* (2000) also about dependencies, exposures, thinking about how our own opacity and unknowing can be the basis of relationality.

29 A model is found in Leonardo da Vinci's *The Virgin and Child with St Anne* (1503–19) where the Madonna bends down towards the Christ child. For Cavarero, 'Leonardo's painting gives the meaning of maternal inclination a special ethical density and a neat geometric linearity' (2016: 99).

30 As Pollock explains, the notion of a 'pathos formula' is drawn from Aby Warburg: 'For Warburg, images are dynamic modes of the transmission of affects. Hence they are formulae for intensity, suffering, abjection, ecstasy, and transformation' (2018: n.p.).

31 Speaking about the coming-of-age story in *Girlhood*, Sciamma comments: 'I thought of Jane Austen, of Jane Campion, of numerous stories where a young girl wants to live her dreams, tries to free herself and comes up against her era, her social and family setting' ('J'ai pensé à Jane Austen, à Jane Campion, à de nombreux récits où une jeune fille veut vivre ses désirs, cherche à s'émanciper et se confronte à son époque, son milieu social et sa famille') (Lalanne 2014: 44). See also Mayer (2015) for discussion of this quotation.

32 Sophie Belot's excellent article on *Water Lilies* (2012: 170) references Akerman's film and takes account of a broader range of female-authored French films about adolescent girls.

33 The title in French, *Portrait de la jeune fille en feu*, also carries echoes of *Portrait de la jeune fille en fleur*, so recalling Marcel Proust's novel of absorption in a band of young girls in love, *À l'ombre des jeunes filles en*

fleur [*In the Shadow of Young Girls in Flower*]. In its English translation, Sciamma's title seems to look out to Henry James's novel of female destiny, *The Portrait of a Lady*, adapted for the cinema by Jane Campion as a work of feminist costume drama in 1996.

34 She says in interview that there is 'the political wish to represent girls, to go into their private worlds, to go into things that are fantasmatic and clinically real all at once' ('la volonté politique de représenter des filles, d'aller dans leurs coulisses, d'aller à la fois dans des choses fantasmatiques et absolument cliniques') (Garbarz and Martinez 2014: 26).

2

Water Lilies

Swimming pools

Sciamma is peculiarly attentive to sensory detail, to what things feel like and how they touch. This attention can be felt through her collaborative work with director of photography Crystel Fournier, who worked on Sciamma's first three feature films. In Sciamma's first feature, *Water Lilies*, Fournier, production designer Thomas Grézaud, and Sciamma create controlled visual environments, bathed in cool colours, blue, turquoise, green, and a nauseous yellow. They share a commitment to a filmic synaesthesia, a sort of sensory overload to carry intense feeling, and to channel rapture and hurt.[1] Feelings are drawn out further in the labile electronic music by artist Para One (Jean-Baptiste de Laubier) that reflects the moods of the films.[2] *Water Lilies*, closes in on the environment of a swimming pool. This story of first love takes as its unlikely subject synchronised swimming. A young girl, Marie, looks longingly at the underwater bodies of the local girls' swim team.

Jean-Marc Lalanne (2007), reviewing *Water Lilies* in *Les Inrockuptibles*, comments on the cinematic aptness of Sciamma's choice to make a coming-of-age movie as her first film. He references films by François Truffaut and Jean Vigo, in the French context, whilst aligning first-filmmaking as art with the act of transition from childhood to sexual maturity. Sciamma has spoken of her interest in American teen movies and of her admiration for directors such as Gus van Sant and Larry Clark, as well as the influence of a filmmaker such as Noémie Lvovsky, whose work shifted cinematic representations of French girls (Lalanne 2007).

Water Lilies is engaged with rapture and transformation. It shows the bruising intensity and gloss of unrequited love, the surface pressure in the blossoming of sexual feeling.[3] It is saturated, bathed in feeling, newly attentive to girls' sensations, its sensorium minutely adjusted to its subject. The space of the municipal pool, with its chlorinated water and bleached, white-tiled surfaces, is a reservoir for the flowering of adolescent girls' eroticism. The public leisure space of the swimming pool is adopted as the stage, the locale, for the film. Sciamma focuses in on intimate relations and observes their propagation in a sterile, showy, wet, public arena.

The pool where Sciamma films is at Cergy-Pontoise in the *région parisienne*. Sciamma's films reference Eric Rohmer's attention to the friendships of young girls and in real world environments, often new town and suburban spaces around Paris. In *My Girlfriend's Boyfriend*, which shows the Cergy pool, Blanche (Emmanuelle Chaulet) gives her new friend Lea swimming lessons. Sciamma's film combines an allusion to Rohmer, documentary realism – this is the town where she grew up – and heightened sense impressions, through a play of colour and light.[4]

Water Lilies opens in the changing rooms of the pool. The camera, at girl height, circles among the swimmers as they dress for their contest, the music of the soundtrack creating a mesmeric effect. The girls rehearse the gestures that will form their aquatic performance. The details here of costume and moves, and intimacy of the shots, are striking. The film's spectacle is foreshadowed, trailed, in this sequence, the light in the changing rooms already anticipating the unreal setting of the pool. Marie, outside, enters the viewing arena where she will find a seat to watch the show. The pool is seen from her angle of vision.[5] The spandex-clad girls emerge in luminous green with sequins and stylised scarlet leaves on their suits.

The first shot of the pool is a beautiful photographic set piece.[6] The water is gleaming turquoise with reflected rose and mauve light in the room. The performers walk in line along the poolside silhouetted against the pink-lit walls and reflected in the pool surface. The appeal of the sequence is heightened by movement, as the girls move gracefully in synchronised sequence along the edge. It is not only the image but its serial motion that captures the eye. The scene unfurls like an early motion study.

In the first performance there are three small girls in glistening water, just their heads above the surface. They are like tiny nymphs. Their performance is very brief, rudimentary, a prelude to the performances of the older teams. *Water Lilies* is not a film of sporting spectacle, and it does not have extended swimming sequences.[7] It is rather a film of mood and feeling, of the lustre that can coat the most quotidian, banal locations. Its adventures are primarily affective.

The film turns from the pool to the domestic bathroom, where Marie, in bathwater, is with her pet miniature turtle, a living creature whose dark prehensile moves contrast with the shining artifice of the pool arena. The white enamel of the bath is seen with Marie's limbs outstretched and the tiny turtle swimming. She practises the moves of the synchronised swimmers, her limbs appearing behind a clear fuchsia shower curtain, recalling the colours of the poolside. The film cuts from this bathroom setting to an external shot of the pool. Marie goes to ask if she can sign up for synchronised swimming. The private space of the domestic bathroom becomes a rehearsal space for the public arena of desire.[8]

Jennifer Barker (2008) has explored the relay between the senses in moments of cinematic excess, drawing on the Silencio scene in *Mulholland Drive* (David Lynch, 2001), a film Sciamma has cited as one of her favourites.[9] Barker draws on Steve Connor (2004), saying 'the senses form an indefinite series of integrations and transformations: they form a complexion' (2008: 238). For Barker, following Connor, 'moments of cinematic, sensory "excess" are sensual reminders of the degree to which vision is entangled with other senses' (2008: 251). In this mix, Sciamma explores further the way longing heightens sense perception, so that the flow of feeling glosses apprehension of the sensory world. This seems anticipated in Connor's image of the senses forming a complexion (a combination of things, and a mood, a colouring). For Sciamma, the inception of sexual feeling brings its own heightening and disorganisation of the senses.

I read this first pool scene as the inception of Marie's love for Floriane, but it is equally possible that this predates the film's diegesis.[10] What is characteristic, lean and bold, in Sciamma, is her attention to moments in the present in her films' narrative that feel instantaneous, like life lived. She does not predetermine how

Figure 2.1 Stills from *Water Lilies* (Céline Sciamma, 2007)

they are encountered, or fix her characters with established stories and histories. She has said that her aim here was to tell the story of what happens before coming out. She says: 'I wanted to make a film about the moment when you feel it in your stomach and you begin to make sense of it, not when it's in your head and you are going to come out' (Garbarz and Martinez 2014: 27).[11]

Water Lilies reveals a moment of heightened receptivity, as Marie knows desire for the first time. Her hyper-acuity and strength of feeling make Marie more open and responsive to the play between the abrasive and the soft, the clean and the abject. The spectacle of first love that emerges, from the pool forwards, is one of intermittence, of hurt and radiance. The sting of chlorine is in the film. Love is shown to be lush and seering. Its intrusions and shape-shifting are part of the intimacy explored.

Mythologies

The object of Marie's affection is Floriane, the leader of the synchronised swim team, her very named associated with flowers and blossoming. She seems to flourish in the early moments of the film. She is first seen as the tallest in an enlaced band of girls posing on the poolside before they start their performance. Floriane's head is poised like a dancer's. She is a queen in this circle. Marie is so absorbed she stays standing up watching the girls and has to be asked to sit down. Floriane's team disappear into churning water, against the sound of Verdi's 'Dies Irae'.[12] In cut-away shots of Marie's face, the shift in her feelings from boredom to rapture is suddenly evident. As the girls emerge from the water, the film closes in on their repeated, echoing gestures and then their metamorphosis as suddenly their legs break the surface. Any sense of the individual is lost as kicking limbs are seen in foam. The girls surface and turn again. The erotic trouble of the image is clear as Marie watches engrossed. Focus on Floriane is delayed and the moment of anticipation seems stretched out.

She is standing, her arm up in triumph, light making the water on her face glisten. She has a nose clip, a detail making her more human. Her smile is radiant, glossy, scarlet. This is the film's first portrait of Floriane and she is exultant, her gesture one of strength. She is seen on the watery background of the pool, its movement and silvery ripples accentuating her miraculous stillness. This fluid setting, her vertical, stretched pose and blondeness, make this image a birth of Venus sequence, gesturing to Botticelli's mythic painting. Floriane is a vision conjured by Marie. She disappears into the water and Marie stands again to applaud. Floriane, out the water, walks on the poolside to join the line of her swim team as their names are read out. Hers is read last. As the name Floriane is heard, she and the girls raise their hands and wave. She waves again, darling, princess, and home-coming queen. The synchronised swimming shots are surpassed by these still and moving portraits of Haenel where Sciamma captures the actress's charisma and photogénie, harnessing them as Marie falls in love. In Book IV of Ovid's *Metamorphoses* the goddess Venus says: 'I, too, have some influence with the sea, for I was once fashioned from foam, in its divine depths' (1955: 108). In *Water Lilies* Floriane seems to emerge and take shape out of the foam of the moving water. She comes up pristine, wet, newly born as a love object.

In her attention to activity and sensation both above and below the surface of the water, Sciamma also recalls stories of naiads, water nymphs in Ovid. As well as the birth of Venus, Book IV of the *Metamorphoses* contains a myth of the origin of coral. Warrior Perseus beheads the Gorgon Medusa (a winged female monster with snakes for hair). Her severed head still has the power to turn whoever looks at it to stone. The touch of her head on living weed in the sea is enough to transform it: 'hardening at the touch of the head, it acquired a strange new rigidity in its leaves and branches' (1955: 114). The text continues:

> The sea nymphs tested this miracle, trying it on several twigs, and were delighted to find the same thing happening again. By scattering seeds from these plants over the waves, they produced more of the substance. Even today coral retains this same nature, hardening at the touch of air: that which was a plant when under the water becomes rock when brought above the surface. (Ovid 1955: 114)

There is a double act of metamorphosis where Medusa's head, cut off, spouting blood, cradled in weed, instates a change of texture and matter. The weed, infested, itself newly metamorphic, changes state between vegetable and mineral as it moves above the surface. The myth draws attention to the repeated trial of this miracle by the sea nymphs.

Julia Kristeva has offered a reading of this passage. She notes: 'Ovid insists upon the petrification of the plants that Medusa's blood transforms into coral' (2012: 29). Playing with the word, she speculates: 'The generic word *coral* could come from *core* [in Greek] which means "young girl", like Medusa; or it might be an allusion to Coré-Persephone, the queen of the dead, to whom the severed head of the Gorgon belongs...' (2012: 29). Her argument runs that this is a drama of the ambivalence of mother–child separation. She says of Medusa, 'this slimy head, surrounded by coiled snake hair, evokes the female sexual organ – the maternal vulva that terrifies the young boy' (2012: 29). Medusa, this figure of castration, only becomes bearable as icon. She is abject in her slime, reminding the boy viewer afraid of the female genitals of 'that archaic nondifferentiation in which there is neither subject nor object, only the sticky, slimy ab-ject' (2012: 31).

Water Lilies, with the reference to a slippery sea creature in the title in French *Naissance des pieuvres* (meaning literally 'the birth of the octopuses'), takes us from octopus to jellyfish, from *pieuvre* to *méduse*, from the birth (*naissance*) of Venus to the state-changing power and horror of Medusa.[13] But Sciamma, beyond Kristeva, thinks female anatomy and sexuality outside a heterosexual dyad and familial frame. She explores the fascination, sensuality and tremor, or girls' desire for each other, and the shifting fear and emotion around this. The mother is out of the frame (there are almost no adult characters in *Water Lilies*). The girls are in the pool alone, as Sciamma rewrites origin myths to fit girl on girl love.

Ovid's nymphs, metamorphic young girls, recalling *core*, the Greek for young girl, and playing with coral, look forward to the scintillating swimmers of Sciamma's film. Corals are not weed as Ovid, and Kristeva, suggest. They are marine animals and they respond to touch. The miraculous transformations of the coral, the sensory rupture in the move from living organism to petrified skeleton, are recalled in a series of sense patterns in Sciamma's film which play out the testing of hard and soft, abrasion and caress.[14]

In its initial attention to the spectacle and accessories of synchronised swimming, the film creates a gritty, abrasive aesthetic.[15] It yields brittle, coruscating sense impressions, where distorted sounds, and patterns of glittering light on the azure pool, match the girls' sequined swimsuits, sprung nose-clips, and gel-slicked hair.[16] Sensual and athletic bodies are seen being exercised, depilated, coated, lacquered. But as Marie also swims underwater in the film, she glimpses a liquid world of headless, swirling, moving bodies, thighs, skin, and spandex fabric. Sciamma reimagines immemorial images of naiads, of swimming girls, of metamorphosis, that speak to the intensity of adolescence and the new strangeness of erotic awakening.[17]

Hurt

A particular issue in erotic awakening Sciamma explores in *Water Lilies* is that of hurt. She is a filmmaker who in her bodily, affective filmmaking pays attention to abrasion, and to vulnerability.[18] Her films conjure the words of Judith Butler:

> The body implies mortality, vulnerability, agency: the skin and the flesh expose us to the gaze of others, but also to touch, and to violence, and bodies put us at risk of becoming the agency and instrument of all these as well. (Butler 2004: 26)

These are the issues Sciamma reflects on, allowing a space for thought and feeling about skin and flesh exposed to the gaze, and also to touch, and violence. As for Butler, so for Sciamma, recognition of the body's exposure is part of a feminist politics that attends to pathos and hurt. Sciamma shows how women and girls can also hurt each other. Attention to singular bodies, their sensory loveliness, their strength, and their susceptibility to damage, to the full gamut of bodily feelings, risks, and violations, is a means of reflecting on domination. Drawing attention to hurt is a way of doing politics through sensuous cinema, through a relay of feelings. The hurt Sciamma shows, and the vulnerabilities she exposes, sharpen responses, deepening feelings.

In this showy film, Marie is in love with Floriane. It hurts. Throughout the film Marie is roughed up, as Floriane maintains a shadow-play of affection whereby she mimes desire for Marie, only to pull away, rendering her suitor defenceless. So Mayer speaks of 'the emotionally violent put-downs of [Marie's] mean girl crush Floriane' (2016: 126).[19] Jean-Baptiste Morain, reflecting on Sciamma's films more broadly, writes in a review of *Portrait of a Lady on Fire*: 'There is also a theme which is very strong in Sciamma's cinema (and in her screenplays for other directors): that of humiliation which can only be fixed by humiliating in turn' (2019: 40).[20] Marie may never succeed in humiliating Floriane – she takes out her feelings on her friend Anne (Louise Blachère) instead – but this powerplay is felt harshly across a series of troubled sequences between the two.

A second bathroom sequence, after Marie's bathing alone with her turtle, comes soon after Marie's second visit to the pool. She is at a party with Anne and other members of the swim teams, male and female. Moving through the rooms, Marie comes across Floriane in a turquoise vest top, her hair picked out in almost chlorinated green light. She looks bored and languorous. She goes into the bathroom to be sick. The acid light of the sequence, the mirrored surfaces, the flare of Floriane's golden hair, recall the sense impressions of the pool.

Floriane flushes her vomit away and washes her face. She cleans her lips and chin with her hands, looking at her own doubled, light-rimmed reflection in the bathroom mirror. Seeing Marie watching her, she questions her abruptly. Marie is seen in profile watching Floriane, and Floriane is seen watching herself. She asks Marie for a piece of gum, and checks her reflection. Floriane, spitting out her gum, reaches close as if to kiss Marie, her mouth open. She asks if her breath stinks. The two faces are in near contact, Floriane's mouth only minutely distant. The scene is coloured by Marie's feelings. The sensory loveliness of the near kiss is followed by the pain of Floriane's question. Through the film's synaesthesia, in this image there is a sense of breath up close, its heat and smell.

Marie is toyed with, as Floriane is in a heartbeat soft and brittle (like the coral), seductive and cruel. This oral teasing continues in the film. Further in, Floriane kisses a windowpane, leaving a lipstick imprint that Marie's lonely mouth presses against.[21] Marie puts her lips abject to an eaten apple she has retrieved from Floriane's garbage. And after their full-mouthed kiss near the close of the film, Marie emerges visibly winded with Floriane's lipstick like bruising round her mouth.

In later pool sequences, Marie is seen trailing Floriane at the leisure complex. When Marie stands at the poolside, Floriane invites her in. She swims underwater and sees the uncommon depths of the pool, the moves of the legs bisected from the upper bodies. In their flexibility, their rapid gestures, their weightlessness underwater, the legs, the tight red torsos, recall living sea creatures. The sound underwater is distorted. This pool space holds an unconscious liquid world of turning bodies. Marie swims freely, her moves setting her apart. Her own sensuality and freedom are captured. The film cuts to Marie showering. The cleansing seems almost a relief after her emergence from the liquid world.

The patterns of the film are pursued as Marie dreams in her room at home, playing with her turtle in its little vivarium. Marie and Floriane develop a strange, abusive friendship as they walk through the various geometric precincts around the new town. The rhythm of their friendship is intermittent, depending on Floriane's moves to attract Marie, to draw her in for her own needs, only the more painfully to let her go. Haenel's performance is intoxicating. Her adored body drips glamour, sensation, as Marie feels the rhythm of her dancing, and watches the gold of her hair. Sciamma shows what things feel like for the first time, the impressions left. Here the film most closely recalls Akerman's *Portrait of a Young Girl in the Late 60s in Brussels*.

Hymen

Sciamma's specific originality and innovation are visible above all in *Water Lilies* in the film's sex scene between Floriane and Marie. In an interview with Sam Ashby, she says: 'I write scenes that I believe haven't been written before. In *Water Lilies*, one girl is deflowering another girl without love, in a clinical way' (Ashby 2012: 10).[22] In the hyper-sexualised environment of the swim team, Floriane is phobic and conflicted about her virginity. She has an unmerited erotic reputation. There is an indication that she is harassed by the coach, who insists on massaging her before a competition. In response she invites Marie to break her hymen so she can sleep with a boy. Floriane lies down in her suburban bedroom and under the covers Marie enters her with her fingers. Floriane registers pain, Haenel's response conveying a sense of the entry, the tear, as physical hurt. The effect for Marie is brutal. Her sensory landmark – experiencing the vastness of the act of entering another girl for the first time, of feeling her inside, the erotic awe, the intact emotion – vanishes in the aftermath of Floriane's lack of involvement and in the immediate arrival of her boyfriend.

In this relay, Marie enters Floriane and is instantly expendable and asked to exit. This breaks their relationship. Viewing it is like a kick in the stomach. The scene recalls earlier instants where Marie has been made complicit with Floriane's dating. Floriane toys with her, drawing Marie on a cord. She has a keen sense of Marie's helpless love, of her susceptibility to the liquid spectacle in the pool. The film's aesthetic strategy is so acute that it charts minutely the intermittence of Floriane's attention. There are moments when the film itself seems lost in Marie's love and enchanted with Floriane's erotic possibility. These times of disavowal make the outcome, the break between them, the more seismic. Sciamma does not demonise Floriane. There are times when she is vulnerable and lovable. Instead, Sciamma shows that for Marie, here, love feels like this.

In her poem 'Ode to the Hymen', Sharon Olds writes: 'How many places in the / body were made to be destroyed / once?' Her words call to mind the strangeness of the hymen, its status as an anatomical anomaly. Where for so many girls the hymen is torn in exercise or sport, or is not there at all, for Olds it is there, and thick tissue. She continues, about its breaking: 'I'd never / felt such pain' (2016: 3). In *Water Lilies*, this breaking of the hymen, this fingering of the vulva by Marie at Floriane's bidding, is a same-sex act where a girl is asked to execute an anatomical rite of passage. The scene finds the exact point where pain subsumes pleasure, as the opening of her vulva offers anguish and then literal pain for Floriane, and as Marie comes face to face with Floriane's lack of reciprocation of her feelings.

If the attention to the removal of the hymen is surprising, the scene has a symbolic power in the film. In remaking a coming-of-age film, Sciamma lets the passage between childhood and adulthood seem like a membrane that must be broken. Her films offer a passing through from an imaginary world of play and infatuation into a new world of the real. This is a way in which she explores transition and metamorphosis. Her films are neither nostalgic for childhood, nor expressly bleak about adult realities and the social world. She has a stringent, honest, and political vision of the intensity of child and adolescent experience, and the pain as well as rapture of growing up. This pain is not numbing but energising, allowing a bid for change and freedom.

If Kristeva reads the encounter with Medusa in relation to the fear of castration, Sciamma dramatising the breaking of the hymen offers a different encounter with female genitals. This piece of tissue is removed so Floriane can live her sexuality and access its different pleasures. At the same time the act, and her agency, give access to a new truth for Marie. Sciamma's filmmaking makes female anatomy a site of versatility, unexpected pain and pleasure, as she will pursue in *Portrait of a Lady on Fire*, her most fully realised love story.

The breaking of the hymen is part of the rupture of Marie's love for Floriane. This is a painful love but it is not formed around the pain Floriane creates. Marie will reckon with it and move on. If the film has created portraits of Floriane, icons of this blonde love object, as it moves to its close, it becomes more fully apparent that its subject throughout has been Marie, her psyche, her desire. At the pool party which makes up the last scene of the film, Floriane is an alluring siren in artificial light. She dances alone, in love with herself.[23] Marie now washes away the lipstick from Floriane's kiss, rinsing her mouth in the water of the pool.

Pauline

The pool is Marie's space, beautiful in the semi-darkness, still with no moving bodies or altered voices. She drops in fully dressed, a descent, a drowning, a cleansing, a rebirth. She swims up and emerges. Her friend Anne comes to meet her and jumps in. The film shows Floriane in a trance, dancing. It cuts to Marie and Anne in the water, their arms outstretched like a star.[24] Their bodies mirror each other, their dark clothes recalling the pet turtle. In the last shot their faces are close, momentarily aligned with one another. Their friendship is intact. Anne's eyes are closed, but Marie's are open.

This floating sequence aligns Sciamma's film with a vision of young girls floating, undoing the vertical world, at the end of Lucrecia's Martel's *The Holy Girl* (2004). In the echoes in her film, Sciamma looks for alternative myths of desire, of girl sexuality, of a female relation to the female body, the fear and tenderness around it. The spaces of her films, the swimming pool, the bathrooms, offer so many arenas for sensory heightening. *Water Lilies* is a film which uses immersion to explore an awakening of desire. In filming desire, Sciamma is attentive to troubles, distractions, disruptions, unpredictable scenarios. She makes these tangible through the sense patterns of her film.

The intermittence of sensation tested by Ovid's sea nymphs is realised in the acrid sweetness of the film, its political attention to a girl's sexuality and its affective intensity. This is a film about love, because it is a film that pays attention to ways in which, with whatever abrasion, Floriane opens Marie's world and reorganises her senses. The film is saturated with feeling. It is not fixed, and offers no protection from fear, sliminess, the abject. It is a film about being undone, by love and grief, about not remaining intact, about the force and beauty of intrusion and metamorphosis. It is a film alive to the ways in which emergent desires, and their interruptions, entering cinema, transform its politics. *Water Lilies* reaches a truce. Marie leaves Floriane behind. Sciamma waits until her next project, a short, to film a happy ending.

Pauline (2010) was part of a commissioned project *5 Films contre l'homophobie* [*5 Short Films Against Homophobia*] based on an idea (and with a script) by Daphné Charbonneau.[25] It stars Anaïs Demoustier as the eponymous Pauline. The film opens with photographs Pauline has stuck on her wall. She explains how she grew up in a small village with her family around. She strokes a cat lying on the bed beside her and the camera slowly pans to the left as she looks round. It follows her horizontal figure, reaching her face. She explains how things began to change when she was fifteen. She describes a feeling of nausea, something growing inside her. The camera is still as she speaks with her head inclined, the film offering a reclining portrait. The pose is one that is like the therapy couch, but also casual, as if she is talking with a friend in her bedroom. The lighting and colours of the shot, her striped shirt, the framing, make this unobtrusively pictorial. Pauline stares into space, and her hand slowly works away at her skin.

She dates a boy, a childhood friend, but leaves him after she speaks about her feelings for girls. She begins to experience taunts and suggestive comments in the village. Demoustier's face registers her shifting emotions. In a long take she talks and she seems to be alone in this space, her lying down part of her sadness. Her monologue tells of what it feels like to be rejected. After *Water Lilies, Pauline* seems to look forward to Marie's future. Pauline is sad because her family do not protect her. She hates herself. She feels all alone. Her parents are ashamed. So Pauline leaves. She says she has not seen them since. It feels as if she is all alone in the world, in the film, in the shot. But, suddenly, this shifts. She says that maybe things will change now. Looking beyond the frame she addresses a 'tu', someone she has been speaking to all along. Adèle Haenel enters the frame, her hand reaching out to Pauline. She is her addressee, her girlfriend. She nestles against her.

Notes

1 I would align her work with Jane Campion's films in this regard, and in particular the immersive and tangible environments of *In the Cut* (2003).
2 See Edney (2020) for a reading which explores the sonorous aspects of the film, suggesting '[t]hrough memory, recognition and association, the music in *Naissance des pieuvres* attaches to the girls; it is these memories that make the soundtrack so effective for fostering links between the spectator and the protagonists' (2020: 290). See also McNeill (2018) on the effect of music in Sciamma.
3 Belot also uses the term 'blossoming' (2012: 172) as she looks at Sciamma's 'lyrical yet realist re-visioning of girls' coming-of-age'.
4 See Belot (2012: 177) for more specific discussion of Cergy-Pontoise, its sites, and its filming by Rohmer.
5 Sciamma has said that she too had 'a revelation on watching synchronised swimming' ('une révélation en voyant de la natation synchronisée') (Garbarz and Martinez 2014: 26).
6 M. Catherine Jonet comments on the visual style of *Water Lilies*, writing: 'she creates protracted, static shots and prolonged cinematic moments that compel the viewer to perceive beyond external appearances. The viewer is invited to take long, lingering glimpses and think over the adolescent characters' actions and choices as well as the filmic elements the narrative presents' (2017: 1127).
7 Clara Bradbury-Rance describes the film 'gesturing towards the sports genre but infusing it with the capriciousness of adolescence' and draws attention to the 'dolphin-like dives of the swimmers' (2019: 81, 85).
8 The bathroom in *Tomboy* is similarly a place of rehearsal of identity.
9 See her *Télérama* interview, 'Céline Sciamma: Il est temps d'écrire pour soi' ['It is time to write for oneself'] (Sciamma 2018), where she also reveals that her childhood bedroom was plastered with posters of Michael Jackson. It was viewing the documentary *Leaving Neverland: Michael Jackson and Me* (Dan Reed, 2019), that inspired Haenel to speak out about her experience of abuse (Dryef 2019).
10 Sciamma likewise offers what is for me an inception, an interpolation, as a child is addressed as a boy in *Tomboy*, but other moments of trans awareness may again predate the action of the film.

11 'Je voulais faire un film sur le moment où c'est dans le ventre et que ça monte à la tête, et non quand c'est dans la tête et que ça va vers le monde.'

12 Bradbury-Rance notes how the film includes 'the spectacle of performance (its opening is accompanied by the extravagant "Dies Irae" from Giuseppe Verdi's *Requiem* [1874])' (2019: 78).

13 In his paper 'Eyes wide open: The trope of lesbianism in *Water Lilies*' given at the Sussex Contemporary Directors Symposium on Sciamma (9 December 2020), Scott Reeser connected the image of the octopus [*pieuvre*] to the reference to the same creature in Proust's *Un Amour de Swann* (*Swann in Love*) where Proust compares Swann's jealousy to an octopus: 'His jealousy, like an octopus which throws out a first, then a second, and finally a third tentacle, fastened itself firmly to that particular moment, five o'clock in the afternoon, then to another, then to another again' (1996: 341) ('Sa jalousie, comme une pieuvre qui jette une première, puis une seconde, puis une troisième amarre, s'attacha solidement à ce moment de cinq heures du soir, puis à un autre, puis à un autre encore') (1989: 279). This places *Water Lilies* in a longer line of literary narratives of unhappy love.

14 Catherine Malabou, referring to Beauvoir's work on myth, draws attention to how '[t]he nymph is that malleable matter that men fashion over and over' ('[l]a nymphe est cette matière malléable que l'homme façonne à l'envi') (2020: 33). Sciamma keeps the image of the nymph, and her plasticity, but explores it in a more autonomous space of female viewing, touch and pleasure.

15 This interest in the gritty, the crystalline, is an unlikely connection to Rihanna whose music is so resonant in *Girlhood*. At the start of the 'Diamonds' music video, Rihanna pushes her hands through piles of diamonds thick as gravel. The rocks run between her fingers. In 2014, at the Council of Fashion Designers of America awards ceremony, Rihanna wore a dress encrusted with 230,000 Swarovski crystals.

16 See Belot (2012: 173) for a different reading of the display of beauty in the film in relation to Baudrillard's work on seduction and artifice.

17 In the history of art, images of the goddess Diana with her nymphs, for example painted by Titian in his *Diana and Callisto* (1556–9), offer precursor images of all female worlds.

18 This is brought out particular strongly in her co-written script with Téchiné, *Quand on a 17 ans* [*Being 17*], where the boys who become lovers literally hit and bruise each other.

19 Bradbury-Rance speaks differently of 'the muted disappointment of unrequited desire (Floriane's reciprocation only occurs in moments of strategic necessity)' (2019: 78).

20 'On retrouve aussi un thème très fort du cinéma de Sciamma (et de ses scénarios pour d'autres cinéastes): celui de l'humiliation qui ne peut être réparée qu'en humiliant en retour.'

21 See also Belot's discussion of the trope of red lips in *Water Lilies* (2012: 178–9).

22 Bradbury-Rance writes that '[t]he girls go through the motions of breaking the hymen, itself an antiquated and irrelevant token of virginity' (2019: 91).

23 Beautiful though these images are, Floriane seems destined to stay in her world in Cergy, voting for Sarkozy.

24 For Bradbury-Rance, 'the star shapes that Marie and Anne make in the water are like propulsions back to childhood' as in this scene they are seen 'in the shared haze of a blue filter' (2019: 95).

25 The collection *5 Short Films Against Homophobia* was produced with French government funds for Canal+; the other films were directed by Xavier Gens and Marius Vale, Sébastien Gabriel, Pascal-Alex Vincent, and Rodolphe Marconi. Few critics have discussed *Pauline*, but it is mentioned positively by Simone Emiliani, who describes the film as 'a heartfelt private diary, a confession to the camera' ('un diario privato a cuore aperto, una confessione a macchina') (2013: 53).

3

Tomboy

Childhood

Steven Bruhm and Natasha Hurley (2004) describe the queer child as the one who does not conform to what they are supposed to be in terms of gender and sexual roles. They write about queer childhoods: 'There is currently a dominant narrative about children: children are (and should stay) innocent of sexual desires and intentions. At the same time, however, children are also officially, tacitly, assumed to be heterosexual' (2004: ix). They speak about the panic that ensues in response to a child's sexuality: '[a]nd nowhere is this panic more explosive than in the field of the *queer* child, the child whose play confirms neither the comfortable stories of child (a)sexuality nor the supposedly blissful promises of adult heteronormativity' (2004: ix). They describe the world of children, their gradual subjugation, in terms in line with the visions of Preciado and Goldin. It is this world that Sciamma invites us to see differently, as she takes children's subjectivity and sociality seriously.

In the same volume, *Curiouser*, Jack Halberstam takes up the issue of the tomboy (the identity named in the title of Sciamma's second feature). He argues that this identity is only sanctioned if temporally bound. He writes:

Tomboyism is punished [...] where and when it appears to be the sign of extreme male identification (taking a boy's name or refusing girl clothing of any type) and where and when it threatens to extend beyond childhood and into adolescence. (Halberstam 2004: 193)

As he puts it: 'the image of the tomboy is tolerated only within a narrative of blossoming womanhood; within such a narrative, tomboyism represents a resistance to adulthood itself rather than to adult femininity' (2004: 194).[1] Kathryn Bond Stockton writes: 'One can remember desperately feeling there was simply nowhere to grow' (2009: 3). The queer child does not see themself moving towards the roles cut and measured socially. She speaks of 'growing toward a question mark' (2009: 3).[2]

The children and adolescents in Sciamma's films are shown headlong in processes of change, transition, and initiation. They are relentlessly, movingly, knocking against the parameters around them. Childhood is reckoned as a time and space of kinesis and change. This is in line with her interest in metamorphosis, and also with her specific take on childhood. In her director interview on the Pyramide Vidéo DVD of *Tomboy*, Sciamma explains that when you film childhood, 'you film something that is disappearing' (2011b).[3] In the equivalent interview, in English, on the Peccadillo Pictures DVD (2011a), she speaks about the crazy energy of childhood, and how that chimed with the short time she had to write and make the film *Tomboy*. She says: 'coming-of-age stories and a young cast allow me to invent my own method and decide who I am, how I want to tell things, how I want to direct actors' (2011a). She shows herself also coming of age as a filmmaker. *Tomboy* was written in a very short period of time and filmed over only three weeks. There is emphasis on change and kinesis.

Sciamma's films are not without their languorous moments, their sense of the timeless idleness of games, of the seemingly unbounded span of the summer holidays, of the ongoing binds to family and a set of relations across time. They hold a very prescient sense of a still time of introspection, reflecting on their characters' consciousness and subjectivity, and on the ways these children are changed and moved. Such moments come often with a stillness of the camera, as a form of portrait is made, as feelings are held, at once intimated and withheld. But if there is a stripe of elegy in her work, its mood refuses nostalgia, idealisation, objectification. Sciamma's work is alive to change and feeds off it. Jean-Marc Lalanne comments to Sciamma that her relation to childhood differs from the melancholy he finds in the films of Gus van Sant or Mia Hansen-Løve (2014: 44).

Sciamma, interested in childhood as it disappears, keeps abreast of this disappearance, toughly, with trenchancy. What Sciamma avoids as far as possible, at least until *Portrait of a Lady on Fire*, is the construction of a child by an adult looking back. The inscrutability of her children is a part of her acknowledgement of their autonomy, of the possibility of lack of access to them. Her first three feature films are about a vivid, immediate reckoning, in the present.

It is in this way that Sciamma's films challenge normative accounts of childhood as both innocent and heterosexual. A challenge of *Tomboy*, her film to date with the youngest children, both characters and actors, is that it acknowledges the complexity of gender and sexuality for children before puberty. It also questions the category 'tomboy', which, as Halberstam has shown, is anodyne only if lived as a stage in girl development. In this film 'tomboy' as name is barely able to contain the depth of feeling, the world-shifting newness of Mickäel's experience. The film, so brief and fleeting, does not follow him far into his future. But it leaves no doubt that whether living as Laure or Mickäel, this child will grow up queer or trans. He will not stay a child or in the family, but emerge into the world.

Sciamma's films are scintillating on account of the intense feeling they conjure, their close apprehension of emotional and sensuous existence. She characterises her screenplays as refusing psychology in favour of action and embodiment (LMC 2016). Her scripts, and the films she imagines and envisages, can thereby come closer to the body, to its intimacy, with few words. She links this limpidity, this interest in action, with childhood and adolescence. This is future-driven and forward-thinking. Sciamma is interested in showing moves to maturity, whilst also attending to the complexity of emotion and social relation of even the smallest children. In *Tomboy* this brings with it a charged questioning of the gender roles available to children, and the possibility of their imperfect enactment.

Critical in this move to work with children and to take seriously their agency, subjectivity and sexuality, is her engagement with actors. Sciamma details her working methods in the director interview of the UK release of *Tomboy*. She explains how important it was that the children really wanted to be part of the film: 'the children would be committed to the parts and the project' (2011a). She speaks of how she worked on 'creating a good relationship with the cast', 'treating them like actors', yet also letting the filmmaking itself becoming a game, letting it be physical. She says that 'you put them really in the scene', 'it's something between you and them' (2011a). As Karen Lury notes:

> Child actors balance precariously on the divide between seeming and being, and they continually undermine the belief that while performing as an actor (playing a character) this performance is held – not necessarily securely but importantly – as distinct from the actor's individual, everyday, off-screen performance of self. (Lury 2010: 151)

In her focus on relationality, on her relations to the children and theirs to each other (the minor child parts in *Tomboy* are played by friends of the main actor), Sciamma achieves an intimacy, a sensory presence, which brings with it some rawness. She moves into the quick of childhood. She reaches to the detail of childhood experiences and also looks beyond childhood towards new futures.

Tomboy has been a groundbreaking film in France, in particular in its use in French schools. In September 2012 it was included in the range of films shown in the initiative 'École et Cinéma' run with the support of the Ministère de l'Éducation nationale and the Ministère de la Culture. It has had a role in particular in advancing debate about the teaching of gender in French schools.

Laure, Laurent, and Mickäel

Tomboy is a film which opens space for questioning gender roles. In interview with Sam Ashby in the queer film magazine *Little Joe*, Sciamma says: 'I remembered that feeling of inventing yourself and playing the boy when I was a child' (2012: 8). She links the film to her own tomboy experience in ways that recall Halberstam, making the acts she shows part of a child's life. 'Playing the boy', being a tomboy, are part of a child's refusal of straight female identity, and of the assumed heterosexuality of girl children. One thing the film does is archive this specific, precious aspect of some lesbian childhoods.

Sciamma suggests that the film is closer to children's reality:

> the movie is not into psychology at all; it doesn't explain why she's doing it, it's all about *how* she's doing it. Kids get that because they can connect to how, because they are still in that phase where they are into imaginary worlds and they think, 'Yeah, I'm Batman', you know? (Ashby 2012: 9)

I take her words not to circumscribe the gender performance as child's play or make believe, nor to limit the film to a lesbian rather than trans reading, but to champion the fluid identifications and gender performances of childhood, and to see these as continuous with an adult world of desire and longing. A brilliant aspect of the film, as Geneviève Morel (2012: 71) points out, is that it allows debate about what is going on.[4]

In a narrative that can read as a trans childhood story, or as a prequel to the same-sex love in *Water Lilies*, Sciamma focuses on tomboy Laure in her first summer in a new suburban neighbourhood. Laure is hailed as a boy by her new girlfriend and love object Lisa. French as a gender-inflected language requires an immediate assumption about gender in any address to the other. Lisa reads Laure as a boy, addresses him thus, and goes uncorrected for the main body of the film.[5] This assumption is arguably necessary to ensure that the attraction straight Lisa feels for Laure is heteronormative. But Lisa's 'grammatical' error meets some desire in

Laure – how long-held this is the film does not reveal – and the act of interpolation allows, or requires, Laure to speak and act with Lisa henceforth as a boy, who is self-named Mickäel.[6] Mickäel exists in the wild spaces and games surrounding the housing blocks he, Lisa, and the other children inhabit. The encounter with Lisa offers a previously unfulfilled self-realisation, whether in a trans identity, in boyhood, in gender fluidity, in lesbian desire, or some combination of these. He keeps this secret from his family.

Sciamma offers a portrait of Mickäel, a boy played by girl Zoé Héran. The careful visual construction of Mickäel bears comparison with that of another cinematic boy character, Laurent, in Louis Malle's *Le Souffle au coeur* [*Murmur of the Heart*] (1971). Sciamma comments to Ashby that she looked at French cinema and coming-of-age films to find the energy of *Tomboy* (2012: 10).[7] Her film follows richly in the line of Truffaut's coming-of-age films and Malle's, and also of Akerman's work as discussed in Chapter 1.[8] Comparison between *Murmur of the Heart*, particularly, and *Tomboy* allows a sense, illusory maybe, that Sciamma's film offers a queer or trans repetition, rehearsal, of certain scenes and poses of Malle's film. The closeness between the images of Laurent (Benoît Ferreux) and Mickäel brings with it the assertion that a girl, or trans boy, can also play the part of the protagonist, the embodied subject, in French coming-of-age cinema.[9] Akerman moved in this direction, finding her passion for cinema through Godard, and filming female protagonists. Sciamma pursues this move further in *Tomboy*.

Murmur of the Heart is an interesting point of reference because it is also a film about adolescent sexuality, using the subject of incest between a mother and son to open a critique of the bourgeois family.[10] Its mood and politics are very different from *Tomboy*, but what it does provide is a schema for thinking about cinematic portraits, showing both the face and the body. Laurent, unwell with the murmur of the film's title, goes to stay in a sanatorium for a cure. The spaces of the sanatorium offer an arena where his body is visible.[11] He is shown with his own reflection in the bathroom mirror, then glimpsed briefly naked as he enters a cubicle for water treatment. His face and torso are seen sprayed with water, in serial and distorting images that seem to reference the multiple identity shots of Antoine Doinel in *Les 400 coups* [*Four Hundred Blows*] (François Truffaut, 1959). And in *Tomboy* the space of washing and bathing, cure and hygiene, is one that is integral to the fashioning of Mickäel as character. It is also familiar as arena in Sciamma's films after her pool locale in *Water Lilies*.

In line with her films' choice of action over dialogue, *Tomboy* is rich with images of Mickäel checking out his own body, including, and beyond, certain bathroom scenes. The start of the film is sensory, showing Laure feeling the wind in her hair as she drives fast in the car with her dad. The short hair here, the bare neck, the breeze, the car, the male bonding, look forward already to Mickäel, and to a shorn, tomboy or boy authenticity. The viewer may also encounter this child as a boy. There is no marker of gender at this stage and this openness seems important for Mickäel's authenticity. This feels like a free, wild start to the film. It also has a point of reference in *Murmur of the Heart*, in a more conventional scene where Laurent is driven by his father to the sanatorium, and the wind plays in his hair.

Tomboy makes the choice to complicate the freedom of its start, offering an image of Laure's body morphology. As Laure gets out of a bath, Sciamma shows her fully naked. Seeing the stretch of her body, its paleness and thinness, is strange. It can feel as if this child is laid bare as a girl as an apparent truth of a sexed body is made visible. The scene raises questions about showing any bare children on film, and about the laying bare of trans and queer bodies. But the discovery that it repeats an image of Laurent bare in *Murmur of the Heart*, further pairing the films, interests me. In this light, I see the scene pursuing Sciamma's deliberate questioning of gender. She makes cinema a space for other morphologies as well as the cis male body. Laure is a new, updated variation on Laurent. The trans boy or queer girl body need not here be read as site of lack or loss.[12] This is a naked image of all that is vivid, quick, unknown, in the body. As Laurent is naked in the sanatorium so is Laure in the bathroom, in scenes that are natural, fleeting, new in cinema, paired by their attention to the body exposed, rather than divided along lines of binary gender.

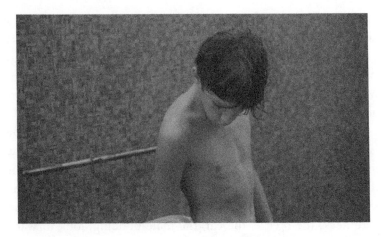

Figure 3.1 Still from *Murmur of the Heart* (Louis Malle, 1971)

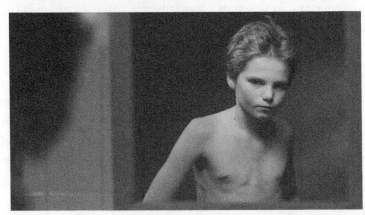

Figure 3.2 Stills from *Tomboy* (Céline Sciamma, 2011)

Later Mickäel is in the bathroom by himself looking at his image in the mirror. The double figure in the frame makes it seems as if there are two children in the space. He surveys himself, lifting up his grey vest, and then takes it off. He examines his own torso. The scene has followed a game of football between the estate children and Mickäel has seen boys play bare-chested. His baring of his torso carries the memory of the scene he has viewed and a glimpse into the future where he too will strip off. He tests himself, checking the image of his chest and ribs. This is a private space and one indoors, away from his family, where he can be freely Mickäel. In closer shots, where the reflection in the mirror takes up more of the frame, Mickäel seems not only to check himself, but now to admire himself, swaggering, and spitting in the sink. This is a portrait scene, a moment where Mickäel can look at himself. He is in an intimate moment on his own as the film draws in close to his feelings and pleasure. He sees how he is read as boy. He takes off his shirt next time he plays football and his body is free. He attracts Lisa's attention bare-chested. His talent at football brings him authenticity.[13]

Mathieu Demy

Sciamma's casting of Mathieu Demy as the father in *Tomboy* is also part of the exploration of a post-binary masculinity. As the son of Agnès Varda and Jacques Demy, Mathieu links Sciamma's work to the heritage of feminist and queer filmmaking in France.[14] He also acted as a child, appearing with particular poignancy as the child Martin in Varda's *Documenteur* (1981). As a father, in *Tomboy*, he brings gentleness and understanding to his eldest child. Their complicity is felt at the start of the film as they play in the car. He brings non-judgemental understanding to Mickäel in the family and in this is in stark contrast to the children's mother (played by Sophie Cattani).[15]

It is a sensitive aspect of *Tomboy* that the father should be much less keen than the mother to uphold binary gender and heteronormativity. By making this choice in the narrative, Sciamma keeps kinship structures and alliance more open and fluid. Within Sciamma's feminism and creation, in *Water Lilies*, *Girlhood*, and *Portrait of a Lady on Fire*, of worlds largely of girls and women, there is a vista in *Tomboy* onto loving masculinity, boyhood, and fatherhood. This is an aspect as well of the narrative in *My Life as a Courgette* which, further than *Tomboy*, moves beyond the nuclear family. Like the source novel, Sciamma's screenplay focuses on children who have for drastic reasons been removed from their families and brought to live in a *maison d'accueil* (a children's home). Courgette has inadvertently caused the death of his mother. Alice has been abused by her father who is now in prison. Camille has seen her father shoot her mother, and then commit suicide. Small figurines, marionettes with large moveable eyes and multiple adhesive expressions, incarnate these children. Sciamma has said that it was Claude Barras's tenderness towards his characters that appealed to her (Caporal 2016). Courgette and Camille are adopted by Raymond, the policeman who first looks after Courgette after his mother has died. A different possibility of intergenerational love and male parental care is imagined in this film. Speaking at the premiere of the film in Paris (on 16 October 2016), Sciamma said she hoped that the film would encourage everyone to welcome (*accueillir*) and adopt each other.

In the nuclear family in *Tomboy* one parent's policing of norms is matched by the other's sweetness.[16] Family intimacy is imaged as close, sensory, unselfconscious. There are scenes where the whole family is seen from a distance, sometimes framed by the spaces of the new house, as if they are figures in a polaroid image or home movie shot. If the film shows closeness between Laure, and then Mickäel, and their father, there is nevertheless no sense that this connection to the father is bound up with the child's gender non-conforming. The film does not tarry with an idea like this. Mickäel's masculinity is not modelled on his father. While the arrival of a 'real' boy, a new baby, at the end of the film seems a harsh blow for Mickäel whose masculinity has been denied and censured by his mother, the film does not pursue a narrative which would see Mickäel responding to either parent's desire for a boy child.[17] Rather Mickäel steps beyond the family.

Jeanne

Sciamma films narratives of queer children and adolescents, Marie, Pauline, Laure, and Mickäel. Yet she also reckons with kids who will, most likely, happily adopt the roles offered by heteronormative society.[18] These kids are also bruised and transformed by the experiences around them. Sciamma's vision shows children and adolescents as ardent subjects, some queer, some not, all impressionable, aching, changing. In films about children and adolescents she has explored a full stretch of feelings of love and hurt.

These emotions are felt with peculiar energy in her filming of siblings. Her siblings are allied and complicit, unspeakably involved with each other, while separate in their own lives. Sciamma tells So Mayer in interview:

> I have a younger sister. To me that's the most intimate part in my films, sibling relationship, and I'm really bad at talking about it, maybe because it's so personal. It's always something I'm obsessed about and I think I will go on talking about that. (Mayer 2015: n.p.)

In speaking about her casting of Héran as Laure and Mickäel, and Malonn Lévana as little sister Jeanne in *Tomboy*, Sciamma explains that what was important was the relationship they could have between them (2011a). She says she 'fell for' Héran and found Lévana 'really cute', 'a very feminine little girl', 'very witty' (2011a). She put them in a room and they started fighting right away.[19]

Critical discussion has centred on Mickäel and *Tomboy* as a film about how to be a boy, about trans childhoods and non-binary gender. Important though this is, it overlooks the focus of the film, as well, on how to be a girl. *Tomboy* is as much a portrait of Jeanne as it is a portrait of Mickäel, and this interest in the little sister, and serious attention to the small girl, her depth of feeling and her social sophistication, are original in the film. Not since Doillon's *Ponette* (1996) has a very young child played such an important role in a French film.[20]

Early sequences in *Tomboy* mark the connection between the siblings and their difference from each other. The family has moved to a new apartment. Laure enters Jeanne's room. A rose-pink curtain, sunshine pouring through, lets the space glow. Jeanne is lying face down on her bed. Plush dalmatians and a baby doll are visible on the shelves behind her. She has heart-patterned sheets, a pink coverlet. Laure sits behind Jeanne and touches her hair.

Play, pretending, and complicity are badged as part of the tender transactions between the siblings. Jeanne sits up and her softness, the sensuality of the curls of her hair, seem accentuated by the warm light of the room. Laure and Jeanne are in their own world. This intimacy is underlined where they are in conversation, closeness showing their fondness for each other. Jeanne tells Laure that she did not bathe and Laure reaches in to smell her skin.

In another scene of the children's downtime with each other, there is a close-up of Jeanne's face with her hands over her eyes. The aesthetic is tactile. She is counting, and missing numbers. The film cuts to her bare feet on the carpet. There is a long shot of her from behind in a pink ballet tutu. She wears this costume with pleasure. As they play hide and seek, Jeanne finds Laure hiding in a cardboard box and runs screaming with joy away from her. Back in the pink bedroom she squeals and collapses on the bed. They romp and fight and nestle and the camera is there with them, in the thick of their play. It is her intimacy with Jeanne that Laure leaves behind as she goes out in the world as Mickäel.

In another scene, Laure is reading to Jeanne from *The Jungle Books*. The film cuts to an image of Laure on the balcony of their flat looking out at boys playing.[21] Jeanne lies alone outstretched in her tutu. She is left behind at this point as Laure goes outside. In subsequent shots she is glimpsed drooping, her body posture belying her depression. Mickäel's love for Lisa displaces his bond with Jeanne. This is illustrated in a direct cut from images of long-haired Lisa in profile running in the woods, to a closer shot of long-haired Jeanne, also in profile, in the bath with Laure.

In the bath Jeanne is doing a rap song about a girl who falls in love. Laure takes the shower attachment as an improvised mike to interview Jeanne. Jeanne plays Jacqueline, an adult star. The colour-scheme is controlled, the girls' skin reflected in the peachy terracotta of the wall tiles. Light reflects off the water on their bodies, and in the porcelain of the bath. Playing with plastic figures leads to a game with dinosaurs and Smurfs. Laure collects up Jeanne's long locks and shampoos them. Jeanne in turn raises Laure's short shampooed hair into spikes. Sciamma shows Laure in a world of play, and then traces her emergence into the world.

From this point on, the film charts gradual shifts in the closeness between Jeanne and Laure. Laure pulls away from Jeanne to become Mickäel as he is drawn into outdoor games with Lisa and other children around the flats. Grief ensues for Jeanne. *Tomboy* is in the quick of experience. The film shows the closeness between the sisters, but does not mourn it as it passes, showing instead different possibilities that open out. These are shown in particular as Mickäel must negotiate his departures from Jeanne.

In a portrait scene in the film, generating the image that is used for publicity material, Laure is drawn by Jeanne. The doorbell rings and it is Lisa. She wants Mickäel to go out and play. Laure takes Jeanne on her lap and explains to her that she is going out.

She moves between Lisa sitting waiting on the steps outside and Jeanne sitting waiting in the apartment. Laure draws a watch onto Jeanne's wrist with a fat felt-tip pen (and later Laure draws a heart on Jeanne's arm). As Laure cuddles Jeanne close to say goodbye, the scale of the shots shows the grief of the scene. There is then a long shot of Jeanne sitting at the drawing table by herself. Mickäel's discovery of boyhood, of Lisa, of a broader world of football, swimming, and dancing leads him away from Jeanne.

Jeanne in turn finds different ways of opening out her love story with Laure. She is watching television by herself with her toy creature when Lisa comes looking for Mickäel. Jeanne immediately realises who Mickäel is. She sits on the hall floor flexing her feet. She later confronts Laure with her knowledge. The siblings do a deal whereby Jeanne too will go out to play. Jeanne now finds a different complicity and intimacy with Mickäel. With infinite flexibility, Jeanne comes up with a story about having a big brother to protect her, adapting suavely to Mickäel. His arrival, if anything, brings them closer.

Going out to play also allows Jeanne to make friends with another little girl Cheyenne (Cheyenne Lainé). While loving Mickäel, she now knows a different relationality. But her knowledge of Mickäel's gender is claimed proudly. She tells Cheyenne, about her big brother, 'he only loved me'. It is a fight after Jeanne has been pushed over that leads to revelation about Mickäel. And it is Jeanne who will comfort Laure on a night of insomnia and grief. Jeanne gets into Laure's bed, taking the initiative to come close to her. She starts a game of Famous People. Laure's first question is 'Is it a woman?' Jeanne replies 'No.' The scene is made up of a long take as Jeanne and Laure play out their game in the semi-darkness, and then Jeanne moves to put her arm round Laure and hold her. The film cuts to a daylight shot of the girls asleep in the single bed.[22]

The intimacy of the relation between Jeanne and Laure, and Jeanne and Mickäel, palpable through the art of the child actors, traced in the sensitivity and imagination of Sciamma's filmmaking, allows a sense of the intensity of love in childhood, its inextricability from later attachments. This is a feminist film which, while exploring queer and trans identities, makes the relation between two siblings its sensory and emotional heart. Love between siblings here queers exclusive focus on exogamous relations in portraying children's emotional lives.

Lisa

In *New Queer Cinema*, B. Ruby Rich connects *Boys Don't Cry* (Kimberly Peirce, 1999) and Sciamma's *Tomboy*, writing: 'Zoé Héran's pitch-perfect embodiment of her private/public gender binarism as Laure/Mickäel make the film's politics of gender dysphoria go down so easily, *Boys Don't Cry* minus the tragedy' (2013: 279). The allusion to *Boys Don't Cry* aligns *Tomboy* with one of the major American indie films about trans identity, transphobia, and homophobia, the film based on the tragic true story of Brandon Teena. Rich points to the way Sciamma's film looks towards different outcomes for the child she shows.

Key in both films is the role of a girl whose interest is bound up with the performance of identity that is achieved. In *Boys Don't Cry*, the role is played by Lana (Chloë Sevigny). Lana chooses love, the truth of who Brandon is, over body morphology. 'No, no, no', she says. 'Button up your pants. Don't show me anything. Think about it. I know you're a guy.' She guides Brandon to look instead at the night sky: 'Look how beautiful it is out there.' Lisa, who first recognises Mickäel and addresses him as a boy, plays a similar role. In both films the girls love the beauty of these trans guys. They are boys, but nicer.

Sciamma says in the French DVD interview: 'the gaze of others defines you' (2011b).[23] This offers a view of portraiture as relational, where the self transforms, and performs, in relation to the other observing. This is key to the portraiture in Sciamma's films, to the undoing of relations of activity and passivity, and the thinking about involvement and exposure. This involvement can be transforming. Lisa's words with the masculine agreement in French, 'are you new here?' ('t'es nouveau?'), interpolate the child in front of her as male. Lisa sees a boy. There is magic in this connection between them because Lisa has seen his truth and seen him as real. Lisa has value for this reason. By recognising Mickäel, Lisa becomes desirable. Lisa is bound up with Mickäel's launching of himself in the world. Being Mickäel is also in some ways about being with Lisa.

Lisa invites Mickäel to her flat. She dances on the bed and he watches her, and then Lisa invites him to dance. The emotions, the sense of fear, the realisation recall Akerman's dance sequence. Lisa and Mickäel dance with a coloured curtain, mauve, pink, turquoise, against the light of the window. They spin and circle holding hands. The words of the love song – 'I love you always' – and their freer and freer movements create an anthem. The film stays with them the length of the song, in elation and freedom. They are breathless and shy when it stops. They are holding hands. Lisa collects her make-up bag and makes Mickäel up as a girl. She touches Mickäel's face with her fingers, smoothing colour onto his eyelids. She takes the chance to touch him. Lisa wants to see Mickäel as a girl. It seems a sign that she has no clue about Laure. She expresses instead, and makes apparent, that it is the girl in the boy that she loves in Mickäel. The scene locates a childish interest in gender fluidity, in dressing up and transformation, that has real meanings for Mickäel.

One of the questions that *Tomboy* raises is whether a relation to Lisa is still desirable or possible with Laure at its close. Sciamma says in interview, 'the end of the film is the end of lying' (2011b).[24] She says: 'the fact of affirming who one is is also affirming the possibility of not having to hide oneself to be who one is' (2011b).[25] She claims the end, where Laure names herself Laure, is 'an act of liberation' and that 'it is not an act of return to the norm' (2011b).[26] Where the end of lying can seem to have positive meaning, Sciamma says in a different interview: 'For me lying is a safety zone of liberty, a space of experimentation, of research and self development, a time bubble where "everything is possible"' (Garbarz and Martinez 2014: 26–7).[27] She speaks about her interest in lies in narrative terms and the alliance between the audience and character created, but her words seem to stretch beyond this implying that there is a particular sense of peace and possibility to be found in suspending full disclosure.

Sciamma's words are open, but it seems the readiest interpretation is that 'who Laure is' in this account is queer. She does not have to hide herself behind Mickäel to love Lisa. The film, in this reading, affirms that possibility of alliance, relation, even romance, between the girls.[28] If Mickäel is a foil, a mask to allow Laure's closeness to Lisa, in the face of homophobia, then there is liberation at the end. The possibility of female–female alliance is a feminist goal here. But that it comes about as a result of the mother's shaming cis agenda and control of her child seems difficult.[29] Some wildness was let out in the film, some aspiration to living and being a true self was unleashed.[30]

Tomboy is a film with competing narratives. It is told quickly, in the quick of experience. It feels real at every turn and adds palpably to the range of French cinema's representations of childhoods.[31] It offers different attachments, different stories – a trans childhood, attraction to a girl, and, above all perhaps, love between siblings. It lets these stories co-exist. It creates a child who exists as a girl, Laure, and as a boy, Mickäel. Sciamma shows how children negotiate binary gender, both controlled by its dictates, and imaginative, aspirational, about change and transition.

Notes

1 See Duschinsky (2014) for a brilliant account which considers *Tomboy* and social constructions of identity, and childhood innocence.
2 See Jonet (2017: 1131) for a reading of *Water Lilies* through Stockton.
3 'filmer quelque chose qui est en train de disparaître'.
4 See English (2019) for readings of this as a film about transgender childhood. Darren Waldron reads the film as a film of gender nonconformity rather than as a trans or lesbian film, writing that 'the film reveals the conditionality of all gendering by highlighting the performative strategies undertaken by boys to comply with compulsory masculinity' (2013: 60).
5 See Morel (2012: 69–70) for a thoughtful discussion of *Tomboy* in relation to Althusser and interpolation.

6 As Laure is seen unpacking her things there is amongst them a cardboard box with a picture of Michael Jackson on it.

7 In the same interview she says that for the style she thought about Gregg Araki's *Mysterious Skin* (2004), David Lynch and comic books (Ashby 2012: 10).

8 Brian Gibson speaks of the 'implicit or even opaque, delicate, often sensual sensibility' of the 'European art film' (2016: 219). Simone Emiliani mentions Claude Miller's coming-of-age films with Charlotte Gainsbourg, *L'Effrontée* [*An Impudent Girl*] (1985) and *La Petite Voleuse* [*The Little Thief*] (1988) (2013: 53).

9 I write this in recognition of the masculine dominance in much New Wave cinema, as explored most importantly in Sellier (2005). I was happy that once Geneviève Sellier was in the audience when I gave a paper on Sciamma.

10 Initially the film was conceived as an adaptation of Georges Bataille's novel *Ma mère*, which was later adapted by Christophe Honoré. See Wilson (2021: 112 n.13).

11 Lucrecia Martel explores a comparable setting in *The Holy Girl* (2004).

12 Mickäel later fashions a penis in playdough to appear in his swimming shorts and this passes as real. If he seems to bow to the pressure to conform to binary gender and male body morphology, fashioning the phallus, and feeling anxiety around peeing standing up, the film shows these fears as the product of a heteronormative world. Mickäel's moments of pleasure, looking at himself, playing with Lisa, allied with his sister, give no sense that he needs a dick to be a boy.

13 Key here too should be a recognition that girls are good at football. Sciamma herself plays football and has spoken of her admiration for US professional footballer Megan Rapinoe.

14 Sciamma speaks about first watching Demy's films when she was a child (Garbarz and Martinez 2014: 25).

15 The relation between trans children and fathers is also explored in films such as *Girl* (Lukas Dhont, 2018) and *Lola vers la mer* [*Lola*] (Laurent Mikeli, 2019).

16 A similar repartition is found between the two masculine roles of Djibril (Cyril Mendy) and Ismaël (Idrissa Diabaté), Marieme's brother and boyfriend respectively, in *Girlhood*.

17 This fear and phobia around trans children and parental desire is addressed with sensitivity in Sébastien Lifshitz, *Petite fille* [*Little Girl*] (2020).

18 If this is the case with Jeanne in *Tomboy*, it was already so with Anne in *Water Lilies*, who is a complex and strongly felt character.

19 Catherine Wheatley, reviewing the film in *Sight and Sound*, writes: 'The central sibling relationship is warm and wonderful, the performances astounding in their naturalism' (2011: 79–80).

20 Levanna also plays in Maïwenn's *Polisse* (2011) but in a more minor role. *Polisse* explores the work of the Brigade de protection de mineurs (the French child protection squad) with Maïwenn herself playing a female detective. For an excellent critical discussion of Maïwenn, see McFadden (2014).

21 Morel points out that *The Jungle Book* is a story of a child living with different species (2012: 70).

22 This is echoed later in *Portrait of a Lady on Fire* as discussed in Chapter 5.

23 'le regard des autres vous définit'.

24 'la fin du film c'est la fin du mensonge'.

25 'le fait d'affirmer qui on est c'est aussi affirmer la possibilité de ne pas avoir à se cacher pour être qui on est'.

26 'un acte d'affranchissement', 'ce n'est pas un acte de retour à la norme'.

27 'Pour moi le mensonge est un sas de liberté, un espace d'expérimentation, de recherche et de développement de soi, une bulle de temps où "tout est possible"'.

28 For Morel, '[the film] suggests [...] that a friendship or homosexual love would have been born between Laure and Lisa' ('[le film] suggère [...] qu'une amitié ou un amour homosexuel serait né entre Laure et Lisa') (2012: 71).

29 Jeri English is tentatively positive about the end, comparing the film to *Ma Vie en rose* (Alain Berliner, 1997) and writing: 'Seemingly, both *Ma Vie en rose* and *Tomboy* end on somewhat optimistic notes: [...] Laure reunites with Lisa under their given name' (2019: 44).

30 Wheatley speaks of 'a glorious summer spent playing football, wrestling with pals and sharing chaste kisses with neighbour Lisa' (2011: 79–80).

31 Gibson is less affirmative than I am, writing: 'Sciamma fetishizes and glorifies the child as forward-thinking and transgressive – the true "trans" of the film – without truly making the child rebellious, while reducing the adult to backwardness and the reactionary' (2016: 220).

4

Girlhood

Mariannes noires

In a Twitter thread from March 2019, Mame-Fatou Niang explains why she thinks *Girlhood*, Sciamma's third feature film, is a 'letdown' for Black France. She sees the film as 'a cinematic beauty loaded with stereotypes and harmful representations', arguing that it needs to be analysed in the context of its production in 'colour-blind' France. She says: 'As a Black French woman, I will never consider *Girlhood* as a movie that represents my experience in France.' She looks to the works of Black French women addressing experiences 'from the inside' and her message is 'please, please, please screen, analyse, work on and cite' Black women. Her own 2016 *Mariannes noires*, made with Kaytie Nielsen, focuses on Black French women, speaking about their understanding of being Black and French, and about their pleasure and pride.[1]

On its release in 2014, *Girlhood* seemed to many critics a phenomenal addition to representations of female adolescence, as a rare work in focus on Black girlhood in contemporary France. So Mayer wrote:

> *Girlhood* is very much a film about the 'hood, an unusual representation of contemporary urban space and its post-colonial subjects as female. The *filles* are banded together by their shared location in the *banlieues* of Paris, with all that that means socially and economically. (Mayer 2016: 137–8)

A point of reference in critical discussions was Mathieu Kassovitz's film *La Haine* (1995), which *Girlhood* followed nearly twenty years later.

Ginette Vincendeau offers a broader context of multiple films that have represented 'non-white segments of the French population' during the years that separate *La Haine* and *Girlhood* (2015: 22).[2] She argues that there has been an incremental increase in French cinema's engagement with social and political issues, and foregrounds the urgency of narratives of multicultural France in light of the resurgence of the Front National. And here one can add, five years on, more recent acts of violence against people of colour in France.[3]

Girlhood is a departure for Sciamma, after two films showing white experience,[4] for its representation of a multicultural *banlieue* community and for her work with Black actors.[5] Interviewed in left-wing French newspaper *Libération*, she spoke of the understanding of intersectionality, of the relation between different struggles against oppression, underlying the film (Péron and Franck-Dumas 2014). *Libération* championed her choices as radical, emphasising the space of representation opened. The paper ran interviews with *Girlhood's* actors and charted the reception of the film in *banlieue* communities around Paris.

In the range of interviews she gave promoting the film, Sciamma acknowledged that this film did not draw on her own immediate experience. In *Les Inrockuptibles* she said that with *Girlhood*, in an inverse move from that found in her first two films, she started from otherness, from alterity, and focused in on the intimate, on intimacy (Lalanne 2014: 44).[6] In an interview with Jonathan Romney in *The Guardian* she says: 'I have a strong sense of having lived on the outskirts – even if I am a middle class white girl. I didn't feel I was making a film about black women but *with* black women – it's not the same.' She continues: 'I just want to give a face to the French youth I'm looking at' (Romney 2015: n.p.).[7] The class issues she implicitly addresses, in French society, in the French film industry, are important. But the equally implicit assumption of identification and commonality of experience, across race, and even across different areas of the *banlieue*, is not straightforward. Sciamma makes a film with Black actresses, and their work is critical to what is achieved as I shall go on to discuss, but beyond their work it is hard to find evidence of participation of other Black artists or technicians in the making of the film. The film remains a vision of Black experience, from another part of the *banlieue*. And, like me, the majority of its viewers and critics are white.

Novelist Léonora Miano in *Habiter la frontière* [*Living on the border*] speaks of the need for representations of Marianne, the personification of the French Republic, to include images of people of colour (2012: 98). She looks at the intersection of gender and race in issues of the representation of the female body, writing:

> the female body generally is even today often still treated as an object … […] the Black body has been the object of too much violence and ostracism for it to be anodyne to treat it like this when one is white and coming from a formerly slave-owning and colonial state. (Miano 2012: 99)[8]

She draws attention to the specific responsibilities of white artists representing the Black body. She continues:

> It goes without saying that people coming out of as painful a history as that of Afro-descendants need positive representations of themselves, of their ancestral history. Questions of the image and of the look seem primordial where they are concerned. (Miano 2012: 128)[9]

And in relation to such representations, Miano asserts importantly that 'one can be Black and French' (2012: 139),[10] despite the persistent association of Marianne and the Republic with whiteness. As pursued in her later *Afropea* (2020), Miano thinks about the Afropean, who has a very particular experience of being born Black in Europe, and envisages Afropean identity and experience allowing a possibility of a post-Occidental era, where white values are not dominant (2012: 140).

Sciamma is a filmmaker who questions the politics of representation of the female body. She is concerned with subjectivity and agency, with children and young women as thinking, feeling, and transforming individuals. Her sensory filmmaking is also attuned to visual beauty, and the spectacle of bodies, their gestures and moves. To cite Vincendeau: 'Sciamma adopts an intensely aestheticizing gaze. *Girlhood* is by her own admission an "impressionistic" tale of youth and her interest is in the choreography of the girls' bodies, the energy of their performances (dancing, fighting), the light on their skin' (2015: 27). Miano's words above imply that whatever Sciamma's intentions and politics, it is not anodyne for her to film the Black body, or to make it part of a spectacle.

Girlhood is difficult, precisely because it pursues some of the same visual and filmic strategies as the previous two films. This is an issue I overlooked when I wrote on the film in an article on 'scenes of hurt and rapture' in Sciamma (Wilson 2017).[11] I am uneasy now about my alignments of the situations of violence, damage, and heartache across Sciamma's first three feature films. If the aesthetics of the films are comparable, the characters have very different histories and contexts, and Sciamma as filmmaker is herself positioned very differently in relation to those histories.[12] Miano's words about violence and ostracism point to what is at stake in making the move from so-called 'alterity' to 'intimacy'. Questions remain about what that passage would involve and how it would be justified, questions which are at odds with French anti-identitarian stances (and with Sciamma's understanding of intersectionality). Sciamma's filmmaking to date has importantly taken stock of a number of concerns in contemporary feminism, including domination and equality, and offers testimony to children's experiences, and to lesbian and trans desire. Her choice to make a film that questions race, exclusion, and opportunity seems in line with her intersectional thinking and recognition that white feminism cannot continue to exclude the experiences of women of colour but it is not uncontroversial.

There has been unease about *Girlhood* as the work of a white French director, and Sciamma as an ally. Arguably the film does not go far enough in responding to and imagining the specific experience of being Afropean in contemporary France. As Niang writes in her monograph, *Identités françaises* (2019):

> Far from being a blank page, the Black body is an entity burdened with a history and with images which make it difficult to universalize its experience. This is not to say that this universalization is impossible, but that all attempt to do so must find its roots in a history of the oppression of these bodies in the West. (Niang 2019: 218)[13]

In line with the words from Miano cited above, Niang's perspective shows the film as insufficiently sensitive to the specific hurt and damage felt transhistorically and in the contemporary moment by young women of colour.[14] For Miano this hurt, this memory of the body objectified (and in history enslaved), corroborated by the range of harmful stereotyped images of young Black women that continue to proliferate in contemporary visual media, means that the stakes are unusually high. Her call is for positive images of young Afropeans, as Niang's is for dissemination of works, and examination of images, imagined and produced by Black women themselves.[15]

I agree with Niang that *Girlhood* structurally and politically lets down the youth Sciamma wishes to give a face to. Sciamma's very wish to grant that visibility is difficult. Response to the film, which is also aesthetically beautiful, and strong in its feminism, is enriched by this admission, or at least an airing of this. I am left with ambivalence about its success. But in what follows I focus on what is positive in the achievement of the film, and on what it may reach towards in its moments of beauty and tenderness. Sciamma did respond to the lack of Black protagonists on film in France. *Girlhood* is at least in some small way part of a journey towards equality and visibility of young Black women in French cinema.

Looking back at *Girlhood*, I ask whether this film also holds positive representations of Black French women and girls. Through its style and success, *Girlhood* has made other once-marginalised kinds of films more visible in the contemporary film industry.[16]

I open questions about whether, in its focus on the characters' dream lives and emotions, its portraits and fantasies, the film may offer a cinematic appeal and sensitivity that its ostensible narrative of a young girl leaving school and home, and becoming involved in violence and drug dealing, seems to occlude.[17]

The opening scene of *Girlhood* shows an American football match at the Stade Léo Lagrange.[18] This prelude is like a fever-dream. Light Asylum's 'Dark Allies' plays over the opening credits, Shannon Funchess singing: 'heartbeats through the dark that spread like a poison / And the tears ran hot like black tar of emotion.' The words draw out sensuality, liquidity. The first image is blurred as helmeted girls run onto the pitch.[19] The shot is thick with the sheen of helmet carapaces, face-mask bars, the rigor of shoulder pads under fabric. The equipment toughens the bodies, accentuating attention to coating and surface. The beat of the music and the pace of the running girls are effortlessly matched. The players seem weightless and elated in artificial stadium lighting. Slow motion shots make the scene unearthly. Girls tackle each other, run, and fall with no damage.

'I'll wait for you, forever / And ever, and ever / And ever.' The song becomes an anthem as a girl runs with the ball. The scene closes as the girls mass, giving high fives, in shots that mingle protagonists with real members of the *équipe* Molosses. The scene works as a pressure vessel for the film, a sensory immersion in feelings yet to come. Like the subsequent 'Diamonds' scene, it is heightened, a part of the dream life of its heroines.[20]

Lycée

In her book *In the Wake*, Christina Sharpe examines the experience of Mikia Hutchings in Georgia. She writes:

> Hutchings and a white friend faced very different disciplinary actions for the same minor incident of vandalism, part of what some see as bias in a state where

> Black girls are five times more likely to be suspended from
> school than white ones. (Sharpe 2016: 122)

Sharpe looks for strategies for making Mikia's point of view visible, offering Black annotations and Black redactions, explanations of history, context, injustice, so that 'we might hear what she has to say in her own defense in the midst of the ways she is made to appear only to be made to disappear' (2016: 122–3). Sharpe makes racist bias and injustice apparent and invites readers, the wider world, to hear the voice of a living, breathing girl. Sharpe writes: 'Aspiration. *Aspiration* is the word that I arrived at for keeping and putting breath in the Black body' (2016: 130). The word holds breath and vision, the possibility of achieving justice and the chance to flourish. This sense of aspiration, life first and foremost, and fulfilment and pleasure, echoes with Miano's call for positive representations.

In *Girlhood* Sciamma, like Sharpe, draws attention to bias in the school system showing this to be present in France, as much as in the US. The trigger for telling the story of Marieme in *Girlhood* is a moment of exclusion. The film takes stock of Marieme's conflicted family situation, where she looks after her younger sisters, and is terrorised by her brother, but shows that the catalyst for change in her life, her coming of age, comes in the failure of the school system. The film cuts from the family home to the public classroom.[21] Marieme is interviewed by a teacher. The girl's face occupies the frame for the whole take. The film offers a series of portraits of Marieme, with no cut-aways to the teacher. This is a serial, living, breathing portrait. It is from the point of view of the white teacher (and cinematographer and filmmaker).[22] But the film's affective focus, its feeling, is with Marieme. It encourages feelings of outrage and entrapment even as it also observes its girl subject. Touré's brilliance as an actress, and the accord and inspiration found in her work with Sciamma, mean that the scene conveys Marieme's emotion, a sense of grief withheld, of dignity and also of disbelief. The film is on her side, and takes her seriously.

The sequence opens with Marieme saying an emphatic no to vocational training. The term she uses is 'CAP' (*certificat d'aptitude professionnelle*) and references the two-year vocational training course at a *lycée professionnel* that is taken in place of the academic *baccalauréat* in France.[23] The teacher argues and is obdurate. Marieme resists, envisaging different outcomes for herself. She is determined and inscrutable, and she shows these qualities later in her work with the girls and as a dealer. Then suddenly, with more evident emotion, she pleads to go into the academic stream. Against her teacher's refusal, she insists that her academic record is not her fault. The teacher ignores her. Marieme pauses. The teacher asks if there is something she should know. Marieme makes no reply. Her silence underscores the need for Black annotation, for recognition that the teacher has failed to open a dialogue with Marieme that would allow her to speak of her aspiration and of the situation – economic precarity, lack of work space, caring duties, family violence – that harms her and holds her back. The school system is shown to have no space for this dialogue and these admissions, and instead replicates a racist division where Marieme is denied any opportunity other than the CAP.[24]

Girlhood shows Marieme aspiring for an academic education and finding this refused at a crucial point in her school career. This is the film's most forceful critique of endemic and structural racism in French society and its implicit, sympathetic understanding that education is one critical part of class mobility and aspiration.[25] Sciamma chooses at this point to sacrifice her character's dreams for an apparent testimony to racism and prejudice in the school system. Romney notes in his interview with the actresses in *Girlhood*:

> As for accuracy, Touré and Sylla [who plays Lady] vouch for *Girlhood* being close to their experience. Like the gang these two have their own stories about shopping with friends and automatically being shadowed by security guards. The same goes for the scene in which Marieme is informed by a teacher that her school grades aren't good

enough for her to graduate to a higher class, even though she's set on pursuing her education. 'It happens to loads of girls', says Sylla. (Romney 2015: n.p.)[26]

A film which makes a different choice is the documentary *Nous, Princesses de Clèves* [*Children of the Princess of Cleves*] (Régis Sauder, 2011), which films students of colour in a French classroom.[27] In the shadow of Sarkozy's highly publicised disdain for the value of counter clerks reading Marie-Madeleine de La Fayette's novel, there is visual power and appeal in seeing schoolgirls learn its words by heart. Close-ups of the student faces convey serious attention. There is delicacy in the sequence, in whispering voices, in images of small butterflies. In *Ouvrir la voix* [*Speak Up*] (2017), Amandine Gay shows an actress rehearsing words from *Phèdre*. In *Mariannes noires* Niang interviews French university professor Maboula Soumahoro and filmmaker Alice Diop amongst other successful professional and creative Black women.[28] Soumahoro speaks of the racism she has experienced, but her example and activism let Niang's film show different possibilities and choices.

Girlhood chooses to show up the failures of the school system but not really to envisage a different future or possibility for Marieme. It chooses rather a different strategy, affirming her instead as a heroine through visual and literary references. The film alludes to the figure of Liberty in a rooftop scene where Marieme is victorious over a rival girl. She is Liberty leading the people, brandishing red fabric.[29] Her name Marieme echoes Marianne, symbol of the French Republic. In another scene, Marieme abruptly forces her way out of a cleaning job by violently locking the arm of the woman supervisor. She is then glimpsed alone, looking out at Paris lights and skyscrapers by night. She is Balzac's Rastignac looking out over the city contemplating his destiny.[30]

The film tells Marieme's story in the terms of French cultural and national heritage, without yet, as in *Children of the Princess of Cleves*, showing her as an active and creative consumer of those artistic and literary sources. There is a bid to see her story as central to France's contemporary narratives. Today's Rastignac is Afropean, and a girl.

But notably the film does not critique the (white) images of nation (Marianne) and class mobility (Rastignac) it references here.[31]

Carrie Mae Weems

In 2019, the Musée d'Orsay hosted the exhibition *Black Models: From Géricault to Matisse*, inspired by the research of Denise Murrell.[32] While the exhibition looked at representations from the nineteenth and twentieth centuries, an important part of its work in Paris involved performance and engagement with contemporary artists, musicians, and writers of colour. Drawing on Murrell's thesis, in the exhibition itself there was emphasis on research to discover the names, identities, and histories of the women and men of colour who worked as models for the artists of this era of modernity. Sciamma's portraits in *Girlhood* are, like so many of the images in *Black Models*, images created by a white artist of Black women and girls. They are lit by a white cinematographer. These are never images 'from the inside' as Niang expresses. Yet as Murrell's work and the exhibition imply, such images are also part of the history of representation of people of colour.

In wondering about the circulation of the images, inspired by Murrell's research into the work of Black models, and also by the idea of collaboration, rather than hierarchy, between artist and muse that Sciamma explores in her later *Portrait of a Lady on Fire*, I am interested in the work of Karidja Touré and how this is critical to the sensitivity of the film. I suggest that it is with Touré, in their work together, in the images they produce, that Sciamma comes closest to being an ally to women of colour, and this partnership is perhaps a source of the positive images of the film that I am seeking, and certainly part of its beauty and *rayonnement*.

Sciamma is interested in offering portraits of young women of colour. She addresses this explicitly in a scene at La Défense where she includes images of the faces of the young women who came to the casting calls for *Girlhood*. But in collaboration with Touré she goes further, her portraits of this young woman part of a sustained, affective project that might be aligned with the portrait art Sciamma makes her subject in her most recent film. In a director commentary on the French DVD (2015), Sciamma speaks about Touré's role in choreographing dance sequences, and also praises the precision of her work in conveying a series of emotions and different feelings as they shift. If it is a risk of the film that Touré's character speaks so little,[33] she is not reduced to an object in *Girlhood*. Her naked body is not exposed. Her portrait is not fixed. She dreams, she feels.[34] She is constantly shifting, opaque and compelling, through Touré and Sciamma's work together. Her imaging, postures, and expressions, in place of words, yield open reflections about poses, subjectivity, and relationality (in ways that recall Cavarero).

My sense of these portraits of Touré as Marieme has been enhanced by looking at photographs by African American photographer Carrie Mae Weems. Her series *Colored People* is

Figure 4.1 Stills from *Girlhood* (Céline Sciamma, 2014)

an artwork which was first created in 1989–90, its title drawing attention to the operation of applying a colour term to a human being.[35] She explores African American skin tones and the language used to describe them.[36] The photographs, toned and colour-stained silver prints, show African American children in shades of blue (and other colours).[37] Two portraits of girls in this series are evocative for thinking about *Girlhood*'s images of Touré. In the first, the girl's head is inclined backwards so her neck is exposed. Her eyes are closed. The calm, the blurred ground, her hair merging into a shadow, her imperviousness to the viewer, speak of reverie. The girl's face is in the sun, its light on her clothing. A blue filter washes the image with memory, melancholy, something unworldly. And the image seems to have cultural associations of jazz, the blues. These feelings settle in a second image of a blue girl where minor adjustments shift the image towards sadness, stillness, and depression. But in both photographs the affective meanings also stay opaque, uncertain.

A similar lability is found in the portraits of Marieme that Sciamma and Touré deliver between them in the film. This is a hidden artwork or project in the film.[38] Sciamma and Touré show Marieme's shifting feelings, her plural identities.[39] This is shown most evidently in the changing frontal shot of Marieme with the teacher, but there is a similar stillness, an almost mesmeric quality, in other images. Sciamma shoots Touré from behind on the housing estate close to the start of the film, showing the light out of the darkness shining on her multiple plaits. Then she is seen head on, her face visible. In the apartment Marieme is with her sisters, quiet and close. Her face is still and melancholy, pained, as she lies prone. Elsewhere she is seen in rapture with Lady, her straightened hair now hanging down. Marieme in different poses is tender to Bébé (Simina Soumaré), her sister, cradling her on her lap, then later standing, her body arched, as the two girls silently say goodbye. There is restraint, secrecy in all these shots as Marieme's feelings run from dream and love, to a winded grief. In Touré's performance Marieme is strong, unstoppable, but she has an aching melancholy. *Girlhood* would not be the same without her. Touré's performance is at its heart.

These images have become visible for me through the work of Weems. These are some of the positive images I find in the film, part of its cinematic beauty. Sciamma believes in pleasure in looking at women, and this is part of her queerness as a director, but she tries to detach this from dehumanising objectification, to make it part of a relay of feeling, of collaboration. Like Cavarero, Sciamma is attentive to the ways different poses hold different emotions and forms of engagement.

As well as offering reflective portraits of Touré, *Girlhood* also shows Marieme existing involved with others. This is the intimacy she claims to reach in the film. The love ties that Marieme feels, to her sisters, to her girlfriends, are, for better or worse, very like those in *Water Lilies* and *Girlhood*. Her inclinations towards her sisters in particular offer images of love, of sorority, of emotional complexity and ethical density.⁴⁰ In looking at them, I am inspired by Weems and in particular her *Kitchen Table* series (1990). Weems's works, multiple images and scenes at the kitchen table, explore her, and other women's, roles and attachments through the return to the same arena of the kitchen and the table at its centre. Sciamma too presents the small family group of sisters in *Girlhood* at a kitchen table.

Marieme comes back after the football match to find Bébé and Mini (Chance N'Guessan) eating their dinner.⁴¹ Their mother has left for work. The older sisters are looking after Mini. Mini chooses a Babybel cheese for her dessert and they let her unwrap it herself, watching as she puts it whole in her mouth. Bébé puts the red wax on Mini's nose, making her a Disney mouse. Marieme washes up as Mini sits on the draining board brushing her teeth. Her profile is highlighted in the neon light. The scene lays out how the girls relate. Marieme is tied in with these sisters. This is their world.⁴²

The love of sisters is one of the closest, most instinctive feelings in Sciamma's films. She shows Marieme and Bébé in their shared bedroom after Mini has gone to bed. Marieme notices that Bébé's breasts have grown and she insists on seeing. Marieme tries to look, Bébé resists, and the film holds their helpless laughter. This is broken as they hear their brother Djibril and both go still. In another scene, after Djibril has been violent to Marieme, back in her bedroom she stares at the ceiling numbly, music on the soundtrack from Para One guiding her feelings. She and Bébé hold hands, their arms stretched out between their beds. Bébé's fingers are pressed into Marieme's palm, with firmness and tenderness.

The representation of the three sisters also allows reflections on Marieme's childhood and on different outcomes she might have known. Marieme's sisters appear at once as characters in their own right and also as variations on Marieme herself, so that her experience at different ages can be sketched.⁴³ In a moment where Djibril holds Marieme in an armlock, Mini can be heard coming into the room, unaware of what is happening. Djibril relaxes and

Mini leaps on him for a cuddle. Sciamma suggests in the film's DVD commentary (2015) that here Marieme remembers her own childhood closeness to Djibril. The image of Mini is full of nostalgia, and also perhaps fear for her future. *Girlhood* displays a series of emotionally complex and beautiful images of Touré as Marieme. Yet in entering the domestic interior of her family, it shows a situation of violence and silencing in which Marieme lives. The kitchen table, the arena of family life where the film assembles its sisters, is also part of a more sorrowful story.[44]

Diamonds

In contrast to its focus on abuse and hurt, *Girlhood* also offers scenes of fantasy and elation. This is its mood at the start in the American football match. The scene of most intense intoxication is the dance to Rihanna's 'Diamonds'.[45] This scene is a fantasy that sustains the film and characters even in their most traumatic moments of the real.[46]

Marieme and the three girls whose group she has joined, Lady, Adiatou (Lindsay Karamoh), and Fily (Mariétou Touré), are in a rented hotel room, a safe space of comfort and luxury where they take bubble baths, eat pizza, and dress up in stolen frocks. Marieme fails to answer calls from her brother. She follows an injunction from gang-leader Lady to switch off her mobile phone.[47] Lady is an alternative authority figure to the teacher, and brother. She tells Marieme that she must do what she wants. She gives her a gold necklace, and renames her 'Vic' as in Victory.[48] Vic dresses up in an electric blue dress, looking at herself with awe despite the heaviness of the security tag on the fabric.

This hotel-room dance sequence is bathed in lush blue light. Sciamma's director of photography Crystel Fournier has commented on the racial dynamics of the lighting:

> we managed to do things we never could have done with white skins. The colour palette we used between blue and

green can produce a gloomy effect and never enhances the actors. But our actresses, since their skin is warm, can handle these types of colours. We could push colours to a point impossible with white skins. (Fournier 2014: n.p.)

This palette is most intense in the 'Diamonds' sequence where vivid blueness coats the whole frame.[49] *Girlhood*'s images are on the side of beauty, the ethereal.[50] They are silvered, 'the blue of vivid dreams and cigarette smoke' (Roth 2004: 159). This is the film at its most aestheticised, as Vincendeau writes. The girls' dancing moves have the same weightlessness as in the opening Molosses shots. The camera is sometimes mobile, moving with them as they dance, moving with the rhythm of the song with levity, nimbleness, ease.[51]

The film cuts to Vic in awe, smiling, moving almost imperceptibly to the music. The camera comes in closer and closer to her face as she watches and listens, her skin shining with reflected blue light, her eyes full of pleasure and grief. Then she too dances in the blue circle of light, stepping into a field of beauty. In this scene, in these moments, the film offers authenticity to the dreams of its protagonists, showing the stretch of their wishes, their imaginary lives. This is a film unafraid of launching a sequence that draws on the energy, glamour, and sheen of the bodies being viewed.[52]

Girlfriends

In *Wayward Lives, Beautiful Experiments*, Saidiya Hartman describes her working method as she undertook her archival and imaginative exploration of Black social life, and of the lives of runaway girls in particular. She says:

I have pressed at the limits of the case file and the document, speculated about what might have been, imagined the things whispered in dark bedrooms, and amplified moments of withholding, escape and possibility, moments when the vision and dreams of the wayward seemed possible. (Hartman 2019: xiv–xv)

Hartman speaks of her book as 'an archive of the exorbitant' (2019: xv) as she looks to conceive of young Black women in the twentieth century as social visionaries and innovators, as sensual and creative, seeking pleasure and beauty. I am inspired by her work as I try to think about what Touré and Sciamma make possible together as they create Marieme, and as they figure her, intermittently, on the side of beauty. I am interested in the potential of the film for thinking about different Afropean destinies, perhaps beyond its own reaches. If it fails to allow these to appear as lived choices, a gesture offered instead in Niang's *Mariannes noires* or Gay's *Speak Up*, the dream life it makes visible at least begins to move in this direction. One aspect of this that Sciamma brings as director, by association if not by design, relates to romance.

Mayer asks Sciamma about Marieme's gender and sexuality: 'In light of your other films, viewers might read Marieme/ Vic as bisexual and/or as trans ... Did you deliberately leave it more open?' (2015: n.p.). In the repertory of scenes and images in the film, there is material that brings a different story, queer and outlaw passions. I choose to see this story existing alongside the straight narrative.[53] A drift of the film is towards attention to women. The first choice Marieme makes is to join up with other girls. The set-up of the film, its visual style, and energy reveal a fascination with their group. The film feels half in love with the girls it shows. This position is sustained in its revelation of what female bonding has to offer Marieme as she claims agency and seeks belonging.

At a rooftop party organised by Marieme's drug-dealer boss Abou (Djibril Gueye), another girl, Monica (Dielika Coulibaly), approaches Marieme and leads her to a spot where they can dance together. The music is louder. Monica and Marieme dancing are tightly framed so they, like the sisters, are in their own world. Monica's hands are round Marieme's back and she hugs her close. The glances between them are grave. The scene is tender. They are dancing slowly. Monica pushes up Marieme's chin and smiles at her. The words of the song are 'Breathe out, breathe in.

It is all ever changing', recalling Sharpe's words, cited above, on breath and aspiration. Even if they are both only seeking refuge from Abou's control, this feels like a moment where a future is imagined. The tenderness and solidarity of the dance lets nothing else exist for a short time. Marieme has with Monica the intimacy she had with her sisters. But then Abou cuts in. As in Akerman's *Portrait of a Young Girl in the Late 60s in Brussels*, the dance is interrupted. Marieme finds the strength to push Abou away, to fight him, and reject his patriarchal control. She refuses submission to him and now exits the life she has created, which has ended up replicating the power dynamic of her family world. The interlude with Monica, this dance, this glimpse of girl love seems to let that happen.

This exit, from family, then from dealing, is affirmed at the end of the film. Marieme presses the entry code for her family's flat and hears Bébé's voice. She hesitates and stays silent. Bébé buzzes the door open, but Marieme lets it close. The pull of the door away from her hand is a physical jolt. The pain of her separation from her sisters, from her girlhood, is registered in the manoeuvre. She finds the strength to let the door close. As in *Tomboy* Sciamma affirms movement on. Marieme walks in the shadow and sunshine of the morning light looking out over the *banlieue* landscape. She weeps. The shots feel heavy with bodily energy. As she slips out of the frame, the film shows blurred, tearful images of trees and tower blocks. But then Marieme steps back into the frame, in focus, taking a breath, closing her eyes, about to run, or dive, into her future.[54] It is the start of a new day. Sciamma leaves Marieme's future unknown.

The film does not give away or imagine what happens next. I wonder what sanctuary or beauty there is for Marieme, what resources she has, what refuge or help she can find with friends, feminists, and activists. I imagine different paths into education, different romantic lives. I want *Girlhood* to be an ongoing riposte to the teacher who shut Marieme out of education. If only in its imaginary afterlives, *Girlhood* shows a girl moving towards a different, dreamed, desired destiny.

Notes

1 I am grateful to Ginette Vincendeau and Sue Harris for drawing attention to the work of Mame-Fatou Niang at the BAFTS Study Day about *Girlhood* in February 2020.

2 Vincendeau makes reference to two films from 2014, *Samba* (Oliver Nakache and Eric Toledano) and *Qu'est-ce qu'on a fait au bon Dieu* [*Serial (Bad) Weddings*] (Philippe de Chauveron), considers films with actors of North African origin, looks at the legacy of *cinéma beur* through directors Merzak Allouache, Rachid Bouchareb and *auteur* director Abdellatif Kechiche, and references attention to France's multi-ethnic population in films such as Claire Denis's *35 Rhums* [*35 Shots of Rum*] (2008) and Jacques Audiard's *Un Prophète* [*A Prophet*] (2009).

3 Régis Dubois (2016: 117–22) offers a different, and damning, appraisal of *Girlhood*. His account of the exoticising language used by the French press to describe the actresses and to convey their sensuality is both revelatory and important (for example, in his charting of the use of animal vocabulary such as 'feline' and 'she-wolf' which he argues constructs Black femininity as physical, wild and violent).

4 The band of children in *Tomboy* includes some kids of colour, but there is little reflection on race in the film.

5 See Frances Smith's excellent volume Bande de filles: *Girlhood Identities in Contemporary France* (2020) for a fuller discussion of the film and its context. For Smith, 'Sciamma's film is alert to the complexities of representation and portraying girls on screen, particularly when they are engaging in spectacular, kinaesthetic activity, like dancing' (electronic edition used).

6 Sciamma's exact words are 'Là, je pars de l'altérité pour l'amener vers l'intime.'

7 Sciamma said in interview: 'I grew up outside Paris too even if I was in a more suburban area. But through the feeling of being on the periphery, that the centre is near but difficult to access, I could reconnect with very strong feelings from my adolescence' ['Moi aussi j'ai grandi en banlieue même si elle était pavillonnaire. Mais sur l'impression d'être à la périphérie, que le centre est proche mais difficilement accessible, j'ai pu me reconnecter à des emotions très fortes de ma jeunesse'] (Lalanne 2014: 45).

8 'le corps féminin, de façon générale, est souvent présenté comme un objet, encore aujourd'hui ... [...] le corps noir a fait l'objet de trop de violence et d'ostracisme pour qu'il soit anodin de le traiter ainsi quand on est blanc, ressortissant d'un pays jadis esclavagiste et colonialiste'.

9 'Il va sans dire que des personnes issues d'une histoire aussi douloureuse que l'est celle des Afrodescendants ont besoin de représentations positives

d'elle-mêmes, de leur ancestralité. Les questions d'image, de regard, semblent primordiales, les concernant.'

10 'on peut être Noir et Français'.

11 I am grateful to B. Ruby Rich for discussing questions about racism at the time I was working on the article.

12 The same is evidently true of the majority white audience and indeed of the majority of critics who have written on *Girlhood*, of which I am one. Hence the importance of the work of a critic like Niang in a field where there are too few Black voices.

13 'Loin d'être une page blanche, le corps noir est une entité chargée d'une histoire et d'images qui en font un terrain délicat à l'universalisation. Ceci ne veut pas dire que cette universalisation soit impossible, mais bien que toute tentative doit s'enraciner dans une histoire de ces corps minorés en Occident.' Niang speaks about 'the deep uneasiness that Sciamma's film has created for numerous Afro-French people' ('la profonde malaise que le film de Sciamma a suscité chez nombre d'Afro-Français') (2019: 208).

14 I am choosing to focus on young *women* of colour, as per Sciamma's arena of representation in *Girlhood*, but as Miano points out in *Marianne et le garçon noir* (2017), the experience of hurt and damage by young men of colour in contemporary France also has its own specificity and history. I am grateful to Ashwiny Kistnareddy for inspiring discussion of these issues.

15 Amandine Gay's film *Ouvrir la voix* [*Speak Up*] (2017) is made up of interviews with young Black women speaking about their self-perception and experiences of racist abuse and discrimination. Its power comes in giving a voice, in letting its subjects be heard. The balance of the individual histories and the broader picture of racism in France is very powerful. The focus on the women as they speak, and the strong alliance between the filmmaker and her subjects, makes the film also seem strongly affirmative and an activist project as well as a work of art. I am grateful to Sophie Niang for recommending it to me.

16 The winner of the Caméra d'Or (prize for the best first feature film presented in any of the Cannes selections) in 2016 was Houda Benyamina's *Divines*, repeatedly compared to *Girlhood* in the press that emerged from Cannes. Benyamina's film is more fluid and less structured than *Girlhood*. Like Sciamma's film it has extraordinary performances from young female actors (Oulaya Amamra and Déborah Lukumuena).

17 Kerensa Cadenas writes: 'With *Girlhood*, filmmaker Céline Sciamma has brought to the screen the delicate, joyful, beautiful coming-of-age story of Marieme (Karidja Touré), a black French teenage girl, who is fed up with her abusive home life … Sciamma's films effortlessly combine beauty, lyricism and a naturalistic storytelling in her direction and narratives. They ache with the care she takes to her craft and the importance of honestly

telling the stories of her characters' (2015: n.p.). In his review, A. O. Scott wrote: '"Girlhood" can be described (like so many movies these days) as a coming-of-age story, and it honors the genre, and its main character, with exemplary sensitivity and sympathy' (2015: n.p.).

18 Sciamma has filmed women from Les Molosses, Asnières-sur-Seine, one of the premier 'American football' teams in France.

19 On the DVD commentary, Sciamma says that there may be hesitation in this opening over whether these are boys or girls, and whether this is France or America.

20 See Pember (2020) for a brilliant, different reading of musical moments in *Girlhood* which closely examines 'Dark Allies' (and 'Diamonds') finding through the politics of the pop music Sciamma cites, melancholy as well as neoliberal resilience, and ambivalent affect.

21 This brief scene in the film merits comparison with other more extended investigations of multiculturalism and the French education system, such as Laurent Cantet's *Entre les murs* [*The Class*] (2008) and Julie Bertuccelli's *La Cour de Babel* [*School of Babel*] (2013).

22 She is played by Aurélie Vérillon, who played a part in Jacques Doillon's film about a small girl mourning her mother, *Ponette* (1996).

23 *Divines* has a memorable classroom scene where girls are given training to become receptionists. As in *Girlhood*, this is a turning point in the narrative and marks Dounia's exit from the school system.

24 *Speak Up* also offers strong perspectives on racism in the school system where academically high-achieving young women also speak of the ways in which they are denied opportunities to progress at school or to access the elite routes into higher education, in particular to the prestigious *grandes écoles* from whose cohorts are drawn future leaders in the private and public sector in France.

25 *Mariannes noires* is affirmative in the way it envisages diverse routes to fulfilment and well-being, in filmmaking, music, hairdressing, running a food company, and so does not only emphasise academic routes.

26 Sylla also puts a question to Romney: 'how come none of the girls succeeds in life'? (Romney 2015: n.p.). Sylla herself has had a successful career as an actress, in film and TV, since the making of *Girlhood*.

27 The location is the Lycée Régional Denis Diderot in Marseille.

28 Maboula Soumahoro is author of *Le Triangle et l'hexagone: Réflexions sur une identité noire* (2020), and Alice Diop has made the films *La Mort de Danton* (2011), *La Permanence* (2016) and *Vers la tendresse* [*Towards Tenderness*] (2016).

29 The reference is to Delacroix's 1831 painting with the same title.

30 The reference is an allusion to the protagonist of Balzac's *Le Père Goriot*, from a comment by Sciamma on the DVD commentary (2015).

31 I am reminded of Miano quoting Audre Lorde: 'The master's tools will never dismantle the master's house' (2020: 87).

32 The exhibition was co-organised with the Miriam and Ira D. Wallach Art Gallery, Columbia University and the ACTe Memorial, Pointe-à-Pitre and shown in the three locations between 2018 and 2019.

33 Where this is a common feature of all Sciamma's films, in *Girlhood* it is difficult since the risk of seeming to silence Marieme's voice is high.

34 For Niang, Sciamma does not manage to 'pierce Marieme's intimacy' ('à percer l'intimité de Marieme') (2019: 230). Perhaps this is ultimately the case, but I feel Sciamma goes further than Niang allows in making Marieme, more than the other more 'stereotyped' figures, the mother, the brother, a complex, moving individual.

35 See <http://carriemaeweems.net/galleries/colored-people.html> (last accessed 12 March 2021).

36 See <https://www.albrightknox.org/collection/collection-highlights/piece: weems-colored-people-series/> (last accessed 12 March 2021).

37 These images appear in her series *Colored People* (1989–90) and in a 1997 exhibition, respectively. See <https://www.albrightknox.org/person/ carrie-mae-weems>;seealso<https://www.albrightknox.org/blog/5womenartists-mendieta-pindell-saar-simpson-and-weems-0> (last accessed 12 March 2021). Carol Mavor, writing on emotion in photography in her study *Black and Blue*, has charted the effect of the images: 'I feel the punch of "Blue Black Boy"' (2012: 42). Mavor is interested here in the emotional effect of photography and writes, vis-à-vis Barthes and Weems: 'Punctum at times may be just a little sting; but when it is coupled with some hard-hitting studium (like the fact of blackness, like the racing of photography, like color and women as nourishing), it is affectively bruising. It makes you black and blue' (2012: 42).

38 The returning images of Touré might be compared to the serial portraits of, for example Hélène Cixous, or Isabelle Huppert, by photographer Roni Horn.

39 As Romney writes: 'on screen, it's Touré's deeply interiorized melancholy that makes her character so enigmatically compelling' (2015: n.p.).

40 Sciamma says: 'The ambition was to show plural female characters, where previous cinematographic examples often confined them to an archetype' ('L'ambition était de montrer des personnages féminins pluriels, là où les expériences cinématographiques précédentes les cantonnaient souvent à un archétype') (Marques 2014: 2). This is addressed most richly perhaps in the characterisation of Marieme's sisters.

41 The casting of Chance N'Guessan as the youngest sister, Mini, seems to recall the casting of Malonn Lévana in a reminder of the earlier child's

appeal. Scenes of intimate care, eating, teeth-cleaning, hair styling, hand-holding, cut across the two films.

42 The interiors were shot in a studio rather than on location, opening some question of whether these are imagined rather than real *banlieue* spaces.

43 This search for a serial portrait across time is found in the photography of Rineke Dijkstra.

44 *Girlhood* displays a feminist impulse to make visible violence against women and girls.

45 Rihanna's 2012 hit 'Diamonds' appears on her album *Unapologetic*. This sequence has drawn many and divergent critical readings. For two readings which look more closely at the significance of sound as well as image, see McNeill (2018) and Pember (2020).

46 The importance of 'Diamonds' to *Girlhood* was drawn out by Gemma Edney in a paper '"Shine bright like a diamond": Rihanna and the transnational experience of girlhood in *Bande de Filles* (Sciamma, 2014)', delivered at the 'Child and Nation in World Cinema: Borders and Encounters in World Cinema' Leverhulme network conference held in Cambridge, UK, 2–3 November 2015.

47 For Isabelle Régnier, 'Céline Sciamma's girls are not revolutionary. They want what consumer society waves under their noses and what France refuses them, but remain subject to the brutal patriarchal order of their neighbourhood' ('Les filles de Céline Sciamma ne sont pas révolutionnaires. Elles veulent ce que la société de consommation agite sous leur nez et que la France leur refuse, mais restent soumises à l'ordre partiarcal brutal de leur quartier') (2014: 21). I think the 'Diamonds' sequence does more than this. Marieme can switch off the phone resisting her brother. The props used in the hotel room are consumer objects, but the dream is for something more and beyond.

48 Vincendeau points out that the name of Vic is 'a reference to the Sophie Marceau character in the 1980 classic French teen film *The Party* (*La Boum*, Claude Pinoteau)' (2015: 27). She cites Sciamma as saying that the original Vic was the perfect little French *fiancée* of the 1980s and that she was looking for the little French *fiancée* of today.

49 I have evoked Carrie Mae Weems in relation to Sciamma's blue colour schemes. Anupa Mistry (2015), in a brilliant piece, draws a different connection to the film work of Hype Williams and specifically to his use of cobalt lighting in *Belly* (1998).

50 See Isabelle McNeill's beautiful, yet more ambivalent reading of luminosity in 'Diamonds' and through the sequence (2018: 337–8).

51 Marieme and Lady also dance later in the film in a sequence choreographed by Karidja Touré. Their outfits recall those worn by the sisters in Jacques Demy's *Les Demoiselles de Rochefort* (1967). Sciamma says in interview that

she grew up in a family where they watched a lot of musicals, Fred Astaire, Gene Kelly (Garbarz and Martinez 2014: 25).

52 For Serge Kaganski, it is an epiphany (2014: 66). Niang writes; 'This hotel scene on a blue background stands out as an extremely strong moment, aided by the beauty of the image and the expertise of the editing' ('Cette scene d'hôtel sur fond bleu se détache comme un moment extrêmement fort, servi par la beauté de l'image et la technicité du montage') (2019: 233).

53 This seems indicated in the music of the film from the start. See Pember (2020: 305) for discussion of the song 'Dark Allies', which she describes 'melacholically investing in queer love, expressing singer Shannon Funchess's love for the female "dark all[y]" of the song's title'.

54 I want to see the end of the film functioning differently from, for example, the end of Lukas Moodysson's *Lilya 4-ever* (2002) where Lilya runs away and jumps from a motorway bridge to her death.

5

Portrait of a Lady on Fire

The artist

Portrait of a Lady on Fire opens with images of different girls' hands as they sketch in charcoal on a white page.[1] Its setting is an artist's studio. It shows a young girl with dark eyes, her hair arranged up, with a plait down the side. She looks up at her model as she draws. Another girl has a delicate muslin scarf at her neck. A third girl has red-blonde hair. A fourth has lustrous pearl pendant earrings. Each head and shoulder shot is like a momentary portrait at the start of the film, with the last image of two girls in the frame, one blurred. The voice of their drawing teacher is heard over the images. She tells them to take time to look at her, and then she herself appears in a reverse shot. She is their subject as she sits, her hands folded. The girls are in a row, poised. The scene is crystalline.[2]

At the start of her period adaptation *The Portrait of a Lady* (1996), Jane Campion includes a sequence of contemporary girls speaking about kissing. Their sensuality colours the film. Sciamma's film begins in period, but with a comparable group portrait.[3] This filmmaker of young girls and children shows a class of girls, pupils of the artist who is the amorous subject of the film. Sciamma focuses on a hidden history of a female painter, and a scene of female education. She marks a continuity between her feminist attention to the affective lives of contemporary children and young women in her other films, and this innovative eighteenth-century drama. She also aligns her own methods, as portraitist in film, with the act of painting she makes the subject of this film, offering momentary portraits of each girl, and opening with a scene of drawing. This studio is the heart of the film, its cradle, this scene postdating the action that then unfolds. In this studio, Marianne (Noémie Merlant) recalls her passion for Héloïse, the young girl, or lady, on fire of the film's title. This hushed space of the studio, with the girls circled around her, is where Marianne casts back her mind, the images flooding.

Sciamma's Marianne is a fictional character, but she is inspired by a flock of women artists in history. The figure to whom she comes closest historically and biographically – the film is set in 1770 – is Elisabeth Vigée Le Brun, portraitist and author of two volumes of memoirs, referenced in the film's credits.[4] Vigée Le Brun, like Marianne, was the daughter of an artist, Louis Vigée, and a prodigious talent. She was official portraitist to Marie-Antoinette, and through her favour became a member of the French Academy (Fumaroli 2015: 31). She fled Paris after the Revolution with her small daughter, and made her living abroad, as a portraitist, in Italy and Russia, before returning to France.[5] Vigée Le Brun's memoirs give no expression of lesbian desire, though speak of her sensitivity to the beauty of her female sitters, which she compliments, as they sit for her, to achieve a finer portrait. Vigée Le Brun found relief and independence abroad away from her husband, the artist Jean-Baptiste Pierre Le Brun, and was deeply attached to her daughter, Julie, nicknamed Brunette, of whom several child portraits exist, including two where she is embraced with her mother, and one where she is half naked, bathing. In her later years Vigée Le Brun enjoyed the attention of her nieces, one of whom was also her pupil.[6]

Vigée Le Brun's memoirs testify to her extraordinary love of art. As she travels through Italy, fleeing France, in every city she arrives in on her way to Rome, she visits the picture galleries and churches. Her appetite for looking, at this moment where she has fled for her life, and witnessed the revolutionary killing of a number of her friends and associates, is intense. On her return to France twelve years later, her first desire is to go to the Louvre

Museum to be with the paintings. She spends so long she is inadvertently locked in and has to hammer on a small door to be let out.[7] This appetite for art and looking, this love of the visual, is what Sciamma carries forward.

Sciamma's film does not draw extensively on the visual style of Vigée Le Brun's portraits in creating the works of her fictional Marianne. But there are remote alliances between Vigée Le Brun's and Sciamma's own visual work in their common sensuality and tenderness, for example the attention to skin and flesh, the velvety textures, and scenes of touch and nestling. Vigée Le Brun and Sciamma also both have a vast talent for representing infants and young women, Vigée Le Brun following the new attention to childhood in Rousseau's wake in eighteenth-century France.[8] She draws her own new-born baby, her daughter as she grows, and the small children of her subjects.[9] *Portrait of a Lady on Fire* draws energy from this instance of a female artist existing independently, through her passion for art and talent, and her transmission of her artistic legacy to female pupils. And Sciamma pursues this feminist line as she demonstrates the relation between the work of women in the visual arts and cinema in France.[10]

Sciamma's *Portrait of a Lady on Fire* is set in 1770, and contemporaneous with the early years of Vigée Le Brun's career, and at a time when other women were also developing artistic careers. Vigée Le Brun herself mentions Rosalba Carriera (1673–1757), the Venetian portraitist and artist in pastels. She also has the opportunity, as she records in her memoirs, to meet Angelica Kauffman (1741–1807), who worked in Rome and London. Another artist referenced by Sciamma and cinematographer Claire Mathon in interviews is Artemisia Gentileschi (1593–1654), who offers scintillating, absorbed portraits of herself painting, an ecstatic Mary Magdalene, a reclining Cleopatra, and bloody visions of Judith beheading Holofernes. *Portrait of a Lady on Fire*, with its fictional artist, offers a vector back to this history of women painting, to the sensations they capture, and their own lived lives.

The film is not tethered to historical detail and veracity, inviting its viewers instead to conjure a more fluid time in the past, to enjoy the novelty and thrill of its vision of women falling in love. Its distinct style, pictorial beauty, clean lines, and simplicity, are carefully created by Mathon, cinematographer, Thomas Grézaud, production designer, and Dorothée Guiraud, costume designer.[11] *Portrait of a Lady on Fire* makes a double move in showing us hidden pockets of the past, drawing on the verifiable histories of women artists, and leading us to imagine new affective and erotic realities for them. The acts of retrieval, and visionary imagining of a mythic time, are both part of a feminist impetus to show at once what was *and* what might have been. It asks us to imagine this story as possible, and creates its own mythic, foundational story of creativity inspired in love between women.[12] It plays in open fields of the imagination, with an array of influences.[13]

In line with this fluidity, Sciamma also moves forward beyond the eighteenth century in the artistic references of the film. Following Vigée Le Brun a couple of centuries earlier, and Nan Goldin in 2010, Sciamma literally made a trip to the Louvre with Mathon. She found herself drawn to images by Corot. *The Bride* (1845) shows a young woman with her hands folded, her melancholy demeanour in the marriage portrait looking out to images of Adèle Haenel. Corot's *Woman with a Pearl* (1870) has a naturalness and sobriety that also bring it closer to the pictorial style of *Portrait of a Lady on Fire*. (Vigée Le Brun's images seem more adorned and ornate in comparison.) Corot's are images from the countryside, not the court. His influence stretches the film forwards into a dreamlike, pastoral future. For Mathon, '[e]ven if it wasn't our period, Corot's portraits inspired us. You have little sense of the direction and colour of the light but rather feel how it brings out the skin tones, the fabrics, the backgrounds' (2019: n.p.).[14] Mathon confirms of her own work in *Portrait of a Lady on Fire*: 'The rendering of skin tones was a primary concern in my work. I looked at once for softness, no pronounced shadows, a slightly satiny rather than strictly realistic feel which is still natural and life-like' (2019: n.p.).[15]

Sciamma also engages with contemporary art by commission-
ing a young woman artist, Hélène Delmaire, to paint the portraits
of Adèle Haenel within the film. This allows the project not
merely to retrieve histories from the archive but to dialogue with a
contemporary woman artist, drawing her work collaboratively into
Sciamma's frame. Delmaire was trained in drawing and painting
(according to nineteenth-century methods) at the Angel Academy
of Art in Florence and works in oils. She frequently takes women
and girls as her subjects, sometimes placing them in lush settings
with plants and flowers. She says in her artist's statement that she
wants to give intensity to 'fragileness' and 'feminine' elements such
as flowers and pastel colours (2020: n.p.). Her loose brushstrokes,
interest in nakedness and in intense states of mind, look outwards to
Lucian Freud's paintings, particularly of his daughters. Delmaire's
work is less intrusive. One defining trait she returns to, and that is
referenced in the film, is the blurring out of an area in a portrait or
nude – the face, the eyes, or the sex – disrupting the reality effect,
as paint, a slash of colour, cuts across the canvas. In a similar gesture
Marianne, Sciamma's fictional painter, smears the painted face on
her portrait of Héloïse.[16] Delmaire explains:

> The subject is often swallowed or hidden by its pictural
> environment; truncated or erased with a swipe of the
> brush. The face and the eyes [...] are turned away or
> masked, turned towards an inner world that can never be
> wholly communicated to another, despite a shared depth.
> (Delmaire 2020: n.p.)

Sciamma's film is committed to a similar vision of portraiture
where, however close the artist comes, however vivid the
rendering of skin and flesh, of the gestures and demeanour of the
model, or beloved, some inner world is withheld. This removal is
tantalising and erotic, as the loved one is never fully touched. It is
also reflective and ethically conscious, as the other always stays,
despite alliance and collaboration, autonomous, ethereal. In the
longing retrospection of the film, as Marianne recalls this love
affair, the sense of remove, of distance, is vital.

Amour

In Hélène Delmaire's painting *Cocoon* (2013), two young girls lie naked on cream silken sheets, one with golden hair, its colour offset by the carmine of her lips. The eroticism of the painting is tender, drawn out in the idle closeness of hands, forearm lying against wrist. This picture is not referenced in *Portrait of a Lady on Fire*, but it foreshadows the film's dalliance with erotic love, its gilded imagining of sexual intimacy, proneness, and reclining.

Marianne is hired to paint Héloïse. This is to be her marriage portrait sent to a suitor in Milan by her noble mother. But Héloïse must not be apprised of this contract. Marianne must work clandestinely, studying her subject with rare attentiveness so she can hold her image in her mind and, once remote, paint her in seclusion. The challenge is extreme, but Marianne meets it and fulfils her commission, only to destroy the image, reveal her secret to Héloïse, and start again in the absence of Héloïse's mother, and with the consent and complicity of her young lady subject. The double staging of the portrait allows the film leisurely time to focus on the act of painting, on the appearance and disappearance of Héloïse's image in paint. Its point is that the painting is a more faithful likeness, a greater token and tribute, with the willing participation of its model. The vision of the film, dependent on balance and equality, favours dual participation of artist and model, and no duality of activity and passivity, of looking and 'to-be-looked-at-ness'.[17]

In this mix comes the dawning of love. Her intent gaze on Héloïse, her learning of her moves and looks by heart, the rapport their glances at each other reveals, lead Marianne inexorably to fall in love with her subject. The second portrait is painted with Héloïse's collaboration, and also with the blush and tremor of love, where painting, the soft tracing in pastel and oil of the loved one's contours, the capture of the light at her throat, is an expression of desire and a prelude to erotic love. The life in the latter portrait derives from the attraction of artist to sitter. The irony is greater that this is a portrait destined to portray Héloïse as lovely and so to arouse the desire of her destined husband.[18] Marianne is so intent on honouring the love that flowers between herself and Héloïse, holding it in paint, and treasuring the proud heroine, that she creates the portrait that will effectively sever their link. As soon as it is finished, Héloïse is whisked away, seemingly vanishing, replaced by her effigy. Her residual appearances in the film, after her marriage, are merely as the subject of another painting, exhibited at the Salon, and as a spectator at the opera, viewed from afar by Marianne.

Painting is Sciamma's subject in this film, but it is also a romance.[19] Although this love is lived out in days, at most a few weeks, calibrated against the painstaking portrait painting, it appears a slow-burning tale, leading by tiny increments to the feminist alliance, and then erotic affair, that becomes possible in the last third of the film. The film is quite chilly in parts, in its lighting, in the cold of the sea water where Héloïse swims, in its rigorous regard for equality, and the seeming equanimity of its heroines. Héloïse at first gives little away, Haenel playing with an inscrutability, a still face, and unwavering gaze, that are starkly different from the moods of her recent roles in French cinema, for Pierre Salvadori or Quentin Dupieux, for example, which have been more casual.[20] The glory of *Portrait of a Lady on Fire* comes in her gradual relaxing, when character and actress give themselves over with a tenderness, intimacy, and trust almost unglimpsed in her other work.[21]

Adèle Haenel starred in Sciamma's first film, *Water Lilies* when she was eighteen. At thirty she plays in *Portrait of a Lady on Fire*. Héloïse has recently left the convent to get married, following her older sister's refusal to marry the same man, and subsequent suicide. Her mother was likewise married to an unknown man, coming to this remote French coastline from Milan, as she says, twenty years before. To be of marriageable age, and her father's daughter, Héloïse is twenty or under. In her strength and demeanour, Haenel's character seems remote from that of an *ingénue* figure educated in a European convent. Comparison with Valentina Cervi's performance as Pansy, Gilbert Osmond's daughter in *The Portrait of a Lady*, only confirms this.[22] In her *Portrait of a Lady on Fire*, Sciamma has Héloïse remember the convent as a space for equality, with a library and music.

Portrait of a Lady on Fire, and its love affair, take place in a small interlude between the convent and ensuing marriage, indenture to an unknown nobleman in Milan. It is a moment where Héloïse can exist outside the law of either church or patriarchy, despite her mother's efforts to uphold the dominion of both. This interlude is where she will know love for the first time. This is a time of a deflowering, and a much happier one than in *Water Lilies*. This is captured in the film as Héloïse and Marianne yield to love, and these are the loveliest parts of this romance. They also feel like a love song to Haenel. The lovers are seen equally, but Haenel's face, her presence, her body, capture attention, respond to the camera. This is apt as these sequences are Marianne's memories of their shared love.

They have a bower, their own cocoon in Marianne's studio in the manor. There is a fireplace, pale panelling, and a deep day bed. Sciamma shows Haenel sleeping here, knocked off the vertical axis, horizontal and unconscious.[23] Her hair is swept up, her cheek pressed against a small pillow and her mouth just slightly open. Her arms are touching, recalling the image in *Cocoon*. She is very still, abandoned, dreaming. Marianne can draw her model now secretly, but in her breathing presence. Their closeness is hushed and erotic, the scene lit by an open fire and candles. The film cuts to a close-up image of Haenel's face on its side, an intimate portrait, rotated and turned sideways. Her lips move almost imperceptibly, as she wakes or dreams. The next shot shows her eyes open as if she has been woken by Marianne's attention. She stays still momentarily, the film in these two near identical shots of her asleep and waking, playing with the movement that is the privilege of the moving image medium, the most tender capture of life, the quickness of the other. From the solipsism and absorption of sleep the film moves to consensual gazing as Héloïse lies back, like Titian's Danaë, receiving Marianne's gaze. She smiles. Marianne continues her sketch.

In a subsequent reclining scene, after they kiss, the film cuts to a shot of Héloïse and Marianne together in the day bed in blue-tinged morning light. They are naked, Marianne curled around Héloïse, their bodies close, aligned and involved, with infinite delicacy. In another scene Héloïse lies back in the white sheets, her blonde hair loose and her breasts bare. The image is casual and natural, though its colours, the gold of her hair, the pink of her lips, conjure a world of divinity, of Botticelli's Venus (recalling *Water Lilies*), Titian's nymphs, or Fragonard's paintings of love. The unselfconsciousness of the actress, her equanimity, make this scene seem to access a further reality beyond the diegesis of the film.

Figure 5.1 Stills from *Portrait of a Lady on Fire* (Céline Sciamma, 2019)

Héloïse has placed a hallucinogenic in a small glass pot on her belly. The green mossy stuff in glass seems to make visible, at one remove, her sex beneath the sheets. Héloïse laughs, flushed. She kisses Marianne's forearm. The joy of the scene is tinged as she says that this will stretch out time, so vital for this love whose lease has all too short a date. Héloïse rubs the plant into her armpit, the gesture, the hairiness, making the act indirectly genital. This is polymorphous perverse sex, all-over body pleasure. A close-up image shows a hand moving under an arm, skin filling the frame. Sciamma creates an unexpected sex act, protects her actresses from genital exposure, and yet captures closely the temporality, the textures, the scent, the humour, of making love.[24] Her lovers kiss sated, as if they have kissed all day, Héloïse now opens drugged eyes, her pupils immense.

The last reclining scene comes on the last night that Héloïse and Marianne will spend together. Héloïse is naked in the daybed, wrapped in a sheet, dreamy, her eyes both open and closed. Marianne makes a miniature of her that she can keep as a love token for memory. Héloïse requests an image by which she in turn can remember Marianne and her lover draws a self-portrait in Héloïse's copy of Ovid's *Metamorphoses*, on page 28.[25] In a further deeply original composition, Sciamma shows Marianne sketching her own reflection from a circular mirror propped against Héloïse's sex.[26] The frame holds Haenel reclining and Marianne's face staring intently from the mirrored surface. Merlant, her dark hair down and tousled, resembles a Medusa figure with snake hair, the round mirror recalling the shield of Athena, goddess of wisdom, which bore the image of Medusa's severed head.[27] Marianne's locks, placed here, make spectrally present Héloïse's pubic hair, while her mouth in the frame makes a small image of Haenel's lips, the face caught in the mirror between Héloïse's legs also speaking of sex. Medusa recalls the death-bearing horror of looking – her gaze turned her objects to stone – and fear of the pilosity of the groin. Yet the image is also demure, an image of the face of the other, a moving reckoning with the strangeness of the other's eyes and lips so near the sex. It is like an optical illusion, a self-reflexive image of the circled involvement of sex, art, memory, loss, and retrieval that the film captures.

In a further shot Haenel reclines on her arm, the image of Merlant reflected still at her sex. Marianne is drawing in the volume of *Metamorphoses*, on page 28. In the portrait that Marianne sees at the Salon, several years later, Héloïse is holding a book open at this same page. This is a romantic sign sent to the other, in the future, of the persistence of love. On the last night before they separate, they lie face to face, equals, sisters staying awake, lovers drinking in each other's image.[28]

Maman

The lovers capture viewers' hearts in *Portrait of a Lady on Fire*, but there are also others in this tiny all-female community in the manor by the sea.[29] Héloïse's Milanese mother, La Comtesse, is played by actress and filmmaker Valeria Golino.[30] Sciamma has a certain disregard for mothers in her earlier films. In *Water Lilies*, parents are missing altogether. Sciamma's Pauline can only exist freely away from her family. In *Tomboy* the mother, pregnant with a new baby, polices binary gender, imposing a female name, girl clothes, and submission to normative laws on her child. In *Girlhood*, Marieme's mother Asma (Binta Diop), who raises her children alone, and works at night as a cleaner in offices at La Défense, is barely present in the film.[31] La Comtesse is marginally more present. Like the mother in *Tomboy*, she demands that her daughter submit to a heteronormative contract (here of marriage), and like Asma in *Girlhood*, who encourages Marieme to take on a cleaning job, by necessity or desire, envisaging her daughter replicating her own destiny.

La Comtesse has attempted to marry her eldest daughter to a Milanese nobleman. The unnamed child has jumped from the cliffs, without a sound, to escape this fate. Her death hangs over the film, her destiny now foisted upon Héloïse who is brought out of the convent to mourn her sister and to fulfil the marriage contract. There is a certain horror in the resumed pursuit of this marriage even as the first child has died, an area that is little explored in the film, but illustrative of its strict verdict on the intransigent mechanisms of heterosexual patriarchy, and the complicity of a certain generation of elite women with this. La Comtesse is in mourning for her daughter, but also melancholy herself on this rugged Brittany coast, away from distraction, company, and cultural life. An insight into her condition comes in a rare intimate dialogue she has with Marianne at a moment when she discovers that this young painter in her household can speak Italian, her mother tongue.

Marianne, like Vigée Le Brun travelling through Italy, is a rare and historically accurate figure of an independent woman supporting herself in eighteenth-century France. She has inherited her father's trade and art as portraitist. Her father painted the marriage portrait of La Comtesse which previously ensured her passage from Italy to France and her destiny in the manor that is the setting of the film.[32] Marianne's independence, and her pursuit of her father's role and profession, allow her symbolically to hold more than feminine value in this household she enters. This is witnessed in early scenes in the film where she raids the kitchens for bread and wine, and smokes by the fireside. She is a gender queer intruder in this house, lightly resembling the visitor to the bourgeoisie in Pier Paolo Pasolini's *Teorema* [*Theorem*] (1968). She drinks with La Comtesse and listens to her story.

La Comtesse and Marianne sit face to face, shown to each other in shot/reverse shot. La Comtesse sits formally in her Prussian blue dress, only its décolleté showing something of her sensibility and sensuality. She slips into Italian, speaking to herself, and Marianne takes up the conversation. Marianne learned Italian in Milan. La Comtesse shares with the artist her urgent desire to return to Milan, motivation over and above social gain, it seems, for her scheming to marry off Héloïse. She entreats Marianne to tell the young girl how beautiful Milan is, how much sweeter life there will be. Marianne retorts that it will be more distracting and pleasant for La Comtesse as well. She accepts this, saying 'certainly' ('certo'), and sits poised, melancholy and unwavering, as Sciamma offers here a brief portrait of a woman of a certain age. Golino's blue eyes are beautifully matched by the colour of her dress, while the shades and textures of her skin and hair are reflected in the fine-grained tan wood of the panels behind her. In exchange with Marianne she reflects on the binds of her own existence and reveals her means, through her power over her daughter, to acquire a different outcome.[33] At the end of the exchange she offers Marianne the chance to take on a further commission, a portrait of one her friends. She then laughs – Golino's naturalness and beauty suddenly clear in the scene. The commission will be difficult because her friend is unusually ugly ('bruta').

La Comtesse is a woman of power and consequence despite her own chattel marriage. Yet she is also a figure of grief who has lost one daughter, and who looks back wistfully at the second whom she perceives still as a child. Marianne spoils the first portrait, smearing the paint across the depicted face of Héloïse. La Comtesse in fury dismisses her as 'incapable', and Héloïse counters her mother's decision announcing that now she will pose. She meets her mother's first desire, that she be painted, by refusing her mother's order that Marianne depart. This throws La Comtesse into confusion. She walks forwards to face Héloïse, the film creating a dual portrait of Haenel and Golino in profile, where they look indeed very credibly like mother and daughter. La Comtesse seeks control, announcing that she will be absent five days and that the picture must be finished before her return. But then in tenderness and sorrow she asks her daughter to say goodbye to her as she used to when she was a little girl (the French is 'petite').

In one of the most beautiful shots of the film, Haenel puts her long hands to her lips, kisses them, and then makes them delicately flutter like butterfly wings landing, with the kiss, on her mother's cheeks. The grace of Haenel's gestures is matched by Golino's intake of breath, her nostalgia for a tiny girl who would kiss her like this. Vigée Le Brun's portraits of Julie are not far. *Portrait of a Lady on Fire* embraces a mother's love for her daughter, its likeness to the love between Marianne and Héloïse, and its relegation as her daughter grows and falls in love. The scene is fleeting.[34]

The mother rigidly ensures her daughter's separation from her lover, and movement onwards to marriage and to Milan. Sciamma takes stock of the entrenchment of La Comtesse herself in a system she works to uphold. It is only in her absence from the scene, in the five days of her travels, the time of the second portrait, that the true liberties and pleasures of the film can be unfurled. In these latter parts, a further character opens and animates the couple forming between Marianne and Héloïse, and this is Sophie (Luàna Bajrami), a maidservant.

Sophie

When Marianne first arrives at the manor she is met by Sophie, who lights her way up the stairs and shows her to her studio. With her white muslin cap, her simple garments, and her extraordinary stillness and composure, Sophie resembles not figures in Vigée Le Brun or Corot, but the young scullery maids and governesses in the domestic scenes of painter Jean-Baptiste-Siméon Chardin. Sophie is the youngest of the four women at the centre of *Portrait of a Lady on Fire*. Bajrami's performance is arresting and the images of her magnetic as the film also offers a portrait of this very young woman. It is Bajrami's second major part after she played the schoolgirl, Apolline, in *L'Heure de la sortie* [*School's Out*] (Sébastien Marnier, 2018). As Apolline, Bajrami has the same stillness and grace she conjures in *Portrait of a Lady on Fire*, but the role of Apolline does not let her show the delicacy, equanimity, and depth of feeling Bajrami displays as Sophie. There are moments which, not advancing the plot, just offer a contemplation of her, at once a portrait and a still life. She arranges a vase of wildflowers and, with her embroidery hoop, catches their likeness in silken threads.

Sciamma pays attention to the young woman whose domestic labour allows the existence in the manor to be pursued. Marianne, an intruder, gender queer and class mobile, is more familiar with Sophie than her mistresses. If Sciamma's feminism draws her to reflect on the lack of freedom of women of different ages, she also, through Sophie, reflects on class difference and feminist alliance. Sophie is not just present in the house, she also becomes closely involved in the story of Héloïse and Marianne, in ways that make the female body central to the film's feminism.[35]

Marianne feels blood coming from her womb and finds refuge in the kitchen where Sophie prepares her a small sack of kernels holding warmth to soothe her pain. As they talk at the kitchen table, Sophie comments that she has not bled for three months. This is unexpected. All men seem to have been absent from this secluded world. Sophie's pregnancy speaks of an outside. She accepts help from Marianne and Héloïse to abort the foetus. Marianne and Héloïse wrapped in their love for one another, in the warmth of new unexpressed erotic feeling – they have not yet made love – take on as their project, in the absence of La Comtesse, rescue of Sophie. They look outwards to the world. The loveliness of their queer desire is intensified, made more possible, physically, psychically, through their feminist alliance with Sophie. Sciamma aligns reproductive rights and freedom to love.

Sciamma shows their endeavours with Sophie pictorially and so, like Jane Campion in the beach scenes between Ada and Flora in *The Piano* (1993), creates frames that speak geometrically of alliance and connection. On the beach in *Portrait of a Lady on Fire*, Sophie, trying to lose her foetus, runs wildly between Marianne and Héloïse, standing far apart, until she drops in exhaustion. The three young women seek medicinal herbs in the sand dunes, emerging out of the long grasses in a sudden triangle. In a third attempt, Sophie hangs from the ceiling, waiting for the force of gravity to work, her feet dangling like a puppet. The surreal image of Sophie suspended, only her lower half in the frame, looks out to more modern artists such as Louise Bourgeois, for whom 'hanging and floating are states of ambivalence and doubt' (cited in Meyer-Thoss 1992: 63). Like this, Sophie's feelings are felt.

This axial experimentation is pursued in the abortion sequence. The alliance of Marianne and Héloïse alone is not enough to deliver Sophie of her unborn child. They find a wise woman (Christel Baras) at a night-time fair, a carnival with women grouped in the firelight and trance-like a cappella singing (arranged by Para One).[36] A pact is made with the wise woman. Marianne and Héloïse agree to accompany Sophie. In the compact timeframe of the days when La Comtesse is absent, Sophie calls them to go with her on the morning after what turns out to be their first night of love. They must rise from one another's arms to be present with her. This rhyming of eroticism and bodily grief is strong. The aura of their love, their female attention to each other, has made possible their feminist support. While their wombs are swollen with love, their bodies having been entered perhaps, felt, Sophie's is sundered by the wise woman, so the foetus will bleed out.

A child lets Sophie into the wise woman's house and helps her unlace her clothes. The cry of a baby is heard as the woman rubs Sophie's hands in ashes. A cut shows Sophie sitting on the bed with two of the woman's children. She lies back recumbent in her chemise, the shot of her prone, in white, copying and varying the reclining shots of Marianne and Héloïse in bed. This is a horizontal image of very different affect, closer to grief and silent protest (recalling Pollock). Sophie is impassive as if on her deathbed with the small children above her. Her knees are raised, her pose resembling the marble woman in Louise Bourgeois's *Femme maison* (1994).

The woman works between Sophie's legs with her prepared potion and Sophie moans, while the baby beside her gurgles. She turns her head toward him. A close shot of Sophie's face shows her agony. The baby, also in the frame, touches her hand, playing with her fingers and reaching for her face. There is extreme pathos in the presence of this tiny child as her foetus is dislodged. The woman's baby, so plausibly there in the overcrowded room, also seems to figure at one remove Sophie's imagining, her lament for a child that might have been. The baby is so tangible in his little jacket, and so jocular as he plays with Sophie. It is a stark new maternity image, a young woman aborting as she is tended by an infant. The child brings tenderness as well as grief into the scene, as living and dying are merged together. Sophie's stillness and equanimity when it is over, her small tears, make this a rite of passage and now she turns to the child. He reaches for her nose and eyes, and she cries. Her face turned sideways is beautiful in glancing light.[37]

Marianne has looked away as the act is carried out, but Héloïse tells her to look and watch. This same impetus to see, and record, is repeated when the young women have returned to the manor. Sophie unwell is nestled like a child under eiderdowns, but Héloïse asks her to get up and makes her lie on a mattress on the ground, now re-enacting the scene so Marianne can paint.

Sophie is laid out in her white chemise, her knees up, Héloïse choreographing her pose, she herself playing the wise woman. The pose is repeated in the neutral setting of Marianne's studio, the traumatic scene a subject in art.

The film seems to allude to that move in late eighteenth-century and early nineteenth-century art to allow painting to become testimonial, seen in the work, for example, of Théodore Géricault. Sciamma imagines visual testimony to abortion far in advance of the feminist filmmaking of Agnès Varda in *L'Une chante, l'autre pas* [*One Sings, the Other Doesn't*] (1977), or of Paula Rego's series *The Abortion Pastels* (1998), made in response to a referendum to legalise abortion in Portugal.[38] Despite this lineage, and the reflection on feminist art's role testifying to the body as site of pain as well as pleasure, the scene is one of the most uncomfortable in the film. Sophie, who was resting in bodily pain and grief, watched over by Marianne, is made to relive her trauma, lying out again, assuming the same position. This comes at the behest of her mistress, Héloïse. Fascination with capturing the image, with art, seems momentarily to over-ride the solidarity with Sophie which has allowed the unwanted pregnancy to be arrested, and the young girl's life to be continued.

Orpheus and Eurydice

This wrestling with art and feeling is central to the film and its ability to leave issues unresolved. In one of the scenes where Héloïse is with Marianne and Sophie, she reads to them exerted passages from Ovid's *Metamorphoses* Book X, the story of Orpheus and Eurydice. Orpheus, accompanying himself on his lyre, addresses the deities of the Underworld, saying he came into their deathly realm because his wife has succumbed, cut off before her prime, poisoned by a viper. The King and Queen of the Underworld are moved by his entreaties and call to Eurydice who is among the spectres newly arrived in the valleys of Avernus. Orpheus may find her again, on condition that he does not look back at her until they have both left the Underworld.[39] To an absorbed Sophie, her face a picture of female education as she listens in the darkness, Héloïse reads aloud. After climbing through the gloom, on reaching close to the surface of the earth, Orpheus looks back and Eurydice slips away. He reaches out to clasp her but touches nothing but the air. Eurydice dies a second time.

The scene allows a moment of rereading and discussion. Sophie finds no reason in Orpheus's actions. The women debate. For Héloïse, he has gone mad in his love. For Marianne he makes a choice, the memory of Eurydice, and so, as she says, makes the choice not of the lover, but of the poet. Héloïse continues to read, describing, from Ovid, Eurydice's fall into the abyss. Then she wonders aloud if it was Eurydice who told her lover to turn and look. Her reading shows the lover curtailing the resurrection and condemning Orpheus to art.

In a scene close to the end of the film, at the Salon, Marianne shows a painting she has made of Orpheus and Eurydice, further emphasising how this story is part of the film's romance. It is a boldness of *Portrait of a Lady on Fire* to reference this myth of love, grief, poetry, and inspiration and to make it central to the love story. This is a retelling of the myth in the feminine. Marianne sees a choice faced for Orpheus between the role of lover who must at all costs retrieve his loved one, and might even stay in the Underworld to love her, and poet who will choose her memory, a subject of his poems. Love and art are seen as intertwined, or severable, distinct.[40]

Portrait of a Lady on Fire is formally made up of a backwards glance, a memory. Its present is the artist's studio where Marianne tutors girls. One girl, played by Armande Boulanger, uncovers in the portfolios of this studio a painting, *Portrait de la jeune fille en feu*, of Héloïse at the night fair with her dress on fire.[41] This picture of conflagration gives the film its title and triggers its memories. The film takes the form of a backwards glance at a lost loved one, so copying Orpheus, and, in Marianne's words, his choice as a poet. It is unclear whether Marianne herself had any other choice but to lose her loved one, but her comments on Ovid show her at least envisaging a choice to be made and art to be her vocation.

The film is also equivocal about whether Héloïse had the chance to make any choice other than the destiny as bride, at her mother's behest, that she submits to. This is a source of argument between the lovers before they part, Héloïse entreating Marianne to find her anything but 'guilty' ['coupable']. The film is mute on whether, in eighteenth-century France, Héloïse without fortune or profession, could indeed have lived independently. More noticeable perhaps is Sciamma's choice to take certain liberties in conjuring this period, while refusing the ultimate anachronism, a happy ending for the female lovers.[42] The film, its romance, is sustained in grief, in line with the pain and rapture of all Sciamma's films.[43]

Portrait of a Lady on Fire is a backwards glance, aligning Marianne with Orpheus the poet. In its form it plays with time, vision, and illusion.[44] Sciamma, together with Mathon, creates a film that in its lighting, its liminal spaces and wild seas, looks back to the classical subjects of Claude Lorrain in the Roman campagna and forwards to the sublime landscapes of Romanticism. Its elemental imaging of darkness, fire, grasses, sand, and the waves of the sea conjures the wildness of nature. The secluded realm is also an Underworld from which Marianne tries to retrieve Héloïse. It is a space of shades and spectres, not only of Héloïse's sister who has jumped to her death, but of Héloïse herself.

Marianne's reveries about the past are severally interrupted by a ghostly image of Héloïse in her bridal dress. It as if the temporal organisation of the film follows Marianne's psyche rather than the sequence of events. The intrusion of this image reveals her haunted by the loss of Héloïse. Her lover is already pictorial, a vision, a shade lost like Eurydice. Reclaiming myths of artistic inspiration, Sciamma imagines her artist as a female Orpheus singing in her art.[45]

The filmmaker says in the Cannes 2019 press release for the film, about her work with Adèle Haenel:

> This collaboration is at the heart of the film which puts an end to the concept of the 'muse' to recount the creative relationship between the viewer and the viewed in a new way. In our studio, there is no muse: there are just two collaborators who inspire each other.

She speaks of the desire for a love story based on equality and takes this further to imagine a relation between artist and subject that is consensual and complicit.[46] It is also the case that Sciamma and Haenel were romantic partners, and that *Portrait of a Lady on Fire* dates from the period after their separation. In 2014, at the César awards, Adèle Haenel thanked Sciamma, 'I would like to thank Céline because, because I love her.'[47] By the time of the interviews after *Portrait of a Lady on Fire* premiered at Cannes, Sciamma speaks of their continuing intellectual dialogue and inspiration.

Coming twelve years after *Water Lilies*, Sciamma's first film starring Haenel, *Portrait of a Lady on Fire* is a backwards glance at Adèle Haenel, a last image of her as a young girl. Sciamma pursues her relations with Haenel in the art they create between them, a film itself about love and art.[48] Even as she puts to an end the concept of the 'muse', Sciamma creates a queer romance of love and filmmaking. This also is part of her feminist legacy, and her almost unique position in contemporary filmmaking as an out lesbian director.

The last images of Haenel are a prolonged portrait in film, a study in emotions. Héloïse sits in a box at the opera listening to the movement 'Summer' from Vivaldi's *Four Seasons*. She is convulsed by the music, flooded with tears, like the Fates hearing Orpheus' singing in the Underworld. This last sequence testifies to the grief of Héloïse as she hears music, which has always been her passion, and as she remembers her love affair with Marianne.[49] This is a portrait of Haenel as an actress. The film celebrates her beauty and her holding of intense emotion, whilst also looking back on her through art. The portrait is a tribute and also a new work of art, a new imagining of feminist filmmaking. Sciamma describes the film to Iris Brey as 'the most joyful thing I've made in my life' (Sciamma 2019).[50]

Notes

1 For Véronique Cauhapé writing in *Le Monde* the film is also a blank page, a new departure for Sciamma (2019: 18).
2 It might be compared with the opening locker room scene with the small community of girls in *Water Lilies*.

3 Iris Brey also connects these two film openings (2020: 87).

4 A retrospective of Vigée Le Brun was held in Paris in 2015. This era of new veneration of women artists, and due attention, is the ground of the film.

5 It should be noted that *Portrait of a Lady on Fire* does not espouse Vigée Le Brun's anti-revolutionary and pro-royalist politics. Instead it makes equality, one of the core values of the Revolution, its guiding concept. In contrast to Vigée Le Brun, her contemporary Adélaïde Labille-Guiard stayed in Paris and served the Revolution (Collective 2015: 83).

6 Xavier Salmon speaks of both Vigée Le Brun and her contemporary, Labille-Guiard, training many female pupils in painting and drawing in the years immediately preceding the Revolution (Collective 2015: 83). One of Vigée Le Brun's pupils, Marie Guillemine Laville-Leroulx, went on to paint *Portrait de Madeleine* [*Portrait of Madeleine*] (1800). See discussion of this painting as an important portrait at the moment of the first abolition of slavery in France (Lafont 2019: 58).

7 It is moving to me that her portraits with her daughter now hang there.

8 See Salmon's brief discussion (Collective 2015: 147). Sciamma names the youngest character in *Portrait of a Lady on Fire*, Sophie, taking the name of the female child whose education Rousseau discusses in *Émile, ou De L'Éducation* [*Emile, or On Education*].

9 Marc Fumaroli sees her as a 'secular heir of the tenderness and anxious happiness of the Italian madonnas' ('héritière profane de la tendresse et du bonheur inquiet des Madones italiennes') (2015: 49).

10 By contrast Agnès Varda, who has responded so powerfully to images in the Western tradition of painting, draws almost entirely on the works of male artists, Titian, Rembrandt, Goya, Picasso, and others.

11 Mathon speaks of creating 'our eighteenth century – or as Céline said our 2018th century' ('notre XVIIIe siècle – notre 2018e siècle disait Céline') (2019: n.p.). Mathon was also cinematographer on Alain Guiraudie's atmospheric queer film *L'Inconnu du lac* [*Stranger by the Lake*] (2013) and, in the same year as *Portrait of a Lady on Fire*, Mati Diop's *Atlantique* [*Atlantics*] (2019).

12 In her 1994 film about a woman artist and female friendship, *Mina Tannenbaum*, Martine Dugowson shows Mina as a child copying Gainsborough's portrait of his two daughters, *The Painter's Daughters with a Cat* (c. 1760), and making the girls turn in to one another tenderly, in another reimagining of eighteenth-century young women. Eighteenth-century painting also inspires Joanna Hogg in the reference to Fragonard's *The Souvenir* (1778) from the Wallace Collection in her film *The Souvenir* (2019).

13 Thomas Sotinel writes in *Le Monde* that this is 'a world out of Breton legends as much as eighteenth-century painting, made of chiaroscuro and dazzling effects, dimly lit interiors and dreamlike visions' ('un monde sorti

aussi bien des légendes bretonnes que de la peinture du XVIIIe siècle, fait de clairs-obscurs et d'éblouissements, d'intérieurs à peine éclairés et de visions oniriques') (2019: 25).

14 'Même si ce n'était pas notre époque, les portraits de Corot nous ont inspirées. On y sent peu la direction et la couleur de la lumière mais plutôt comment elle fait ressortir les carnations, les étoffes, les fonds.' Salmon also speaks in fact of Vigée Le Brun's rendering of 'skin tones, fabrics and other substances' ('les carnations, les étoffes et les autres matières') (Collective 2015: 97).

15 'Le rendu des carnations a été primordial dans mon travail. J'ai recherché à la fois de la douceur, pas d'ombres marquées, un rendu un peu satiné et non réaliste qui reste naturel et extrêmement vivant.'

16 In a new painting for the cover of the Criterion Collection edition of *Portrait of a Lady on Fire*, pale pink paint slashes across the face of Adèle Haenel playing Héloïse in her signature emerald green dress. The paint is the exact colour of the lettering on the title of the film.

17 Sciamma says in interview with Iris Brey, 'equality is the big project of the film' ('c'est le grand projet du film l'égalité') and she speaks of 'the continual surprise' ('la surprise permanente') of equality (Sciamma 2019). Alice Blackhurst writes: 'Sciamma has suggested that one of the "key manifestos" of her film is to thoroughly dismantle the enduring trope of the passive muse, dismissed by the director as a "pretty word" which "conceals women's participation in art history"' (2019: n.p.).

18 For Sotinel, the portrait shows Héloïse 'destined for motherhood' ('destinée à la maternité') (2019: 25), which is certainly borne out as a later portrait of her which is seen at the Paris Salon shows her now with a golden-haired child.

19 Blackhurst's review (2019) is an important feminist appraisal of the film in these terms.

20 Haenel starred as Yvonne Santi in Salvadori's comedy crime drama *En Liberté* [*The Trouble with You*] (2018) and as Denise in Quentin Dupieux's comedy horror film *Le Daim* [*Deerskin*] (2019).

21 Anthony Lane also remarks on a certain shift in *Portrait of a Lady on Fire*. Where he says of the film that now and then it 'acquires the dryness of a tract', he comments as well on its tactility, continuing: '[i]t couldn't be fresher if it were mixed on a palette in front of us, and the intensity with which, in the second half, the women look themselves into love, as it were, is fleshly, funny, and sublimely *un*theoretical' (2019: 79). Jean-Baptiste Morain questions: 'Why is it then that the film is a bit disappointing? It is a bit lacking in flesh, eroticism, letting go' ('D'où vient alors que le film nous déçoive un peu? Il lui manque un peu de chair, d'érotisme, de lâcher-prise') (2019: 40). Jean-Philippe Tessé in *Cahiers du cinéma* writes *Portrait of a*

Lady on Fire off as 'a poor telefilm of bombastic academicism' ('un pauvre telefilm à l'académisme ronflant') (2019: 43).

22 Henry James's novel, as further emphasised in Campion's feminist reprise of its tale, shows the ways in which the convent education Pansy has received, and her apparent purity, do not prevent her falling in love and finding means to escape her father's control.

23 Reclining shots of Haenel, with different affect, are seen in the deflowering scene in *Water Lilies*.

24 She says in interview with Iris Brey: 'I really conceived the film like a new device to give us new sensations, new emotions' ('j'ai réellement conçu le film comme un nouveau manège pour nous donner de nouvelles sensations, de nouvelles émotions') (Sciamma 2019).

25 This page number became a code and meme associated with the film, drawn as skin art on Haenel's forearm as she appeared in interviews at Cannes 2019.

26 Brey, evoking this scene, describes Haenel stretched out like Olympia in Manet's painting of the same name (2020: 64).

27 The most famous image of this is by Caravaggio, *Medusa* (1597) in the Uffizi Gallery in Florence. If Medusa imagery was already there in my reading of *Water Lilies*, *Portrait of a Lady on Fire* shows Sciamma engaging directly with this figure of fear and pleasure.

28 The scene recalls the bedtime moments in *Tomboy* where Jeanne comforts her sibling.

29 As Sotinel remarks, the world of the film is 'a microcosm inhabited by only four characters, who suffice to reveal all the flaws dividing humanity' ('un microcosme habité par seulement quatre personnes, qui suffisent à ouvrir toutes les failles divisant l'humanité') (2019: 25).

30 Golino has acted in other French films, notably working with Valeria Bruni Tedeschi in *Les Estivants* [*The Summer House*] (2018). In casting an Italian actress and creating an Italian mother, Sciamma follows in a line from Chantal Akerman who casts Lea Massari as the mother of her protagonist Anna in *Les Rendez-vous d'Anna* [*The Meetings of Anna*] (1978), creating an extraordinary bedroom conversation between mother and daughter.

31 In Maïmouna Doucouré's *Mignonnes* [*Cuties*] (2020), more attention is given to the subjectivity of a mother, as she undergoes the experience of waiting for her husband to take a second bride, and her daughter's love and fear for her. She tries to police her daughter's behaviour, but at the end of the film sets her free, allowing her not to attend the husband's wedding.

32 In creating the setting of the film the exteriors were filmed first in Brittany, and then the interiors in the manor were shot in a chateau in Seine-et-Marne.

33 In her screenplay for *Being 17* Sciamma explores the subjectivity of a mother watching over the brief love between her son and his first boyfriend, proving, like La Comtesse, sometimes more allied with the lover than the son.

34 Vigée Le Brun's daughter Julie fell in love at seventeen while they were settled in Russia, making a marriage of which her mother disapproved, and filling the artist with grief at the loss of her daughter's companionship.

35 Leslie Felperin notes: 'some may feel Sciamma strays into anachronism just a touch, creating a glimpse of an idealized, classless matriarchal utopia that's more wishful thinking than realist storytelling. But it's still a beautiful dream' (2019: n.p.).

36 Baras is Sciamma's casting director. She also cast Haenel in Christophe Ruggia's *Les Diables* [*The Devils*] (2002).

37 A scene this recalls is the Pietà in Ingmar Bergman's *Viskningar och rop* [*Cries and Whispers*] (1972). In this film the servant Anna (Kari Sylwan), whom Sophie resembles, and who also has space and subjectivity in that period film, holds her dying mistress in her arms. Mathon recalls: 'We rewatched some films by Bergman who knew magnificently how to film women with a unique proximity and intimacy' ('Nous avons revu certains films de Bergman qui a su magnifiquement filmer les femmes avec une proximité et une intimité singulières') (Mathon 2019: n.p.).

38 Brey points to the ways in which the scene shows up the stark lack of images relating to the specificity of female embodied experiences (2020: 86).

39 My summary here draws on Mary Innes's translation (Ovid 1955: 225–6).

40 Sotinel, drawing together the Underworld of Ovid and the fire that is rife in the film, writes that in Sciamma's film 'you have to build your paradise, however fleeting, in hell itself' ('Dans la version que propose Céline Sciamma, c'est aux enfers même qu'il faut construire son paradis, fût-il éphémère') (2019: 25).

41 Boulanger acted in the second series of *The Returned* (2015), the TV drama about the return of the dead on which Sciamma worked for a time.

42 I am grateful to dissertation student Ryan Montgomery for inspiring these thoughts.

43 In H.D.'s poem 'Eurydice', Eurydice questions, in terms that seem to look forward to the images of Sciamma's *Portrait of a Lady on Fire*: 'what was it you saw in my face? / the light of your own face, / the fire of your own presence?' (1982; available at <https://www.poetryfoundation.org/poems/51869/eurydice-56d22fe6d049d>, last accessed 28 March 2021). She laments that Orpheus has returned her to the Underworld, dead again, and in her questioning of their encounter sees it as also challenging, chimerical, agonistic, opening new vistas on the exchange between Marianne and Héloïse in *Portrait of a Lady on Fire*. I am grateful to Xinyi

Wang, who is working on film and mythology, for drawing my attention to the poem.

44 For Felperin, it is 'an exquisitely executed love story that's both formally adventurous and emotionally devastating' (2019: n.p.).

45 For Morain, Sciamma explores 'art as consolation' ('l'art comme consolation') (2019: 40).

46 Agnès Varda, in *Jane B. par Agnès V.* [*Jane B. by Agnès V.*] (1988), explores the relation between a female filmmaker and female muse, but they do not fall in love. See my discussion of this film (Wilson 2019: 75–98).

47 'je voudrais remercier Céline parce que, parce que je l'aime'.

48 For Blackhurst, 'the reimagining of Héloïse as collaborator with her own discrete sense of agency is lent further gravitas by Sciamma's longstanding romantic involvement with Adèle Haenel' (2019: n.p.).

49 Felperin speaks of her experiencing 'a tempest of emotions' (2019: n.p.). Lane describes 'ungovernable sobs, with smiles breaking through like shafts of sunlight' (2019: 79).

50 'la chose la plus réjouissante que j'ai faite dans la vie'.

Bibliography

Alexander, Ella (2014), 'Nan Goldin finds her Eden', *Vogue* UK, 31 March, <http://www.vogue.co.uk/article/nan-goldin-interview-eden-after-photography-book> (last accessed 11 March 2021).

Ashby, Sam (2012), 'Céline Sciamma', interview with Céline Sciamma, *Little Joe* 3: 7–11.

Barker, Jennifer (2008), 'Out of sync, out of sight: Synesthesia and film spectacle', *Paragraph* 31.2 (July): 236–51.

Beauvoir, Simone de [1949] (1985), *Le Deuxième Sexe*, Paris: Gallimard.

Belot, Sophie (2012), 'Céline Sciamma's *La Naissance des pieuvres* (2007): Seduction and be-coming', *Studies in French Cinema* 12.2: 169–84.

Blackhurst, Alice (2019), 'The defiant muse', 22 December, *LA Review of Books*, <https://lareviewofbooks.org/article/the-defiant-muse/> (last accessed 11 March 2021).

Boulé, Jean-Pierre and Ursula Tidd (eds) (2012), *Existentialism and Contemporary Cinema*, New York and London: Berghahn Books.

Bradbury-Rance, Clara (2019), *Lesbian Cinema after Queer Theory*, Edinburgh: Edinburgh University Press.

Brey, Iris (2020), *Le Regard féminin: Une révolution à l'écran*, Paris: Éditions de l'Olivier.

Brinkema, Eugénie (2006), 'Celluloid is sticky: Death, materiality, metaphysics (in some films by Catherine Breillat)', *Women: A Cultural Review* 17.2: 147–70.

Bruhm, Steven and Natasha Hurley (eds) (2004), 'Introduction: Curiouser: On the queerness of children', in Steven Bruhm and Natasha Hurley (eds), *Curiouser: On the Queerness of Children*, Minneapolis, MN and London: University of Minnesota Press, pp. ix–xxxviii.

Butler, Judith (2004), *Precarious Life: The Powers of Mourning and Violence*, London: Verso.

Butler, Judith (2005), *Giving an Account of Oneself*, New York: Fordham University Press.

Cadenas, Kerensa (2015), 'An interview with Céline Sciamma, Director of *Girlhood*', *Jezebel*, 3 February, <http://themuse.jezebel.com/an-interview-with-celine-sciamma-director-of-girlhood-1683367053> (last accessed 11 March 2021).

Caporal, Alexandre (2016), 'Interview: Claude Barras et Céline Sciamma pour *Ma vie de Courgette*', 4 July, <http://www.daily-movies.ch/interview-claude-barras-celine-sciamma-vie-de-courgette> (last accessed 11 March 2021).

Cauhapé, Véronique (2019), 'L'Esquisse d'un amour', *Le Monde*, 21 May, p. 18.

Cavarero, Adriana (2000), *Relating Narratives: Storytelling and Selfhood*, London and New York: Routledge.

Cavarero, Adriana (2016), *Inclinations: A Critique of Rectitude*, Stanford, CA: Stanford University Press.

Chevalier, Karine (2019), 'Repetition and difference: The representation of youth in the films of Céline Sciamma', in Romain Cahreyron and Gilles Viennot (eds), *Screening Youth in Contemporary French and Francophone Cinema*, Edinburgh: Edinburgh University Press, pp. 62–80.

Clouzot, Claire (2004), *Catherine Breillat: Indécence et pureté*, Paris: Cahiers du cinéma.

Collective (2015), *Elisabeth Louise Vigée Le Brun*, Paris: Éditions de la Réunion des musées nationaux – Grand Palais.

Collective (2019), *Le Modèle noir de Géricault à Matisse*, Paris: Flammarion.

Connor, Steve (2004), 'Intersensoriality', talk given at a conference on The Senses, Thames Valley University, 6 February, <http://stevenconnor.com/intersensoriality.html> (last accessed 11 March 2021).

Delmaire, Hélène (2020), 'À propos', <https://www.helenedelmaire.com/pages/a-proposabout/> (last accessed 11 March 2021).

Despentes, Virginie (2006), *King Kong Théorie*, Paris: Grasset.

Dryef, Zineb (2019), 'La Société des réalisateurs exclut Christophe Ruggia', *Le Monde*, 6 November, p. 23.

Dubois, Régis (2016), *Les Noirs dans le cinéma français: De Joséphine Baker à Omar Sy*, La Madeleine: Éditions LettMotif.

Duras, Marguerite (2014), *Le Livre dit. Entretiens de Duras filme*, Paris: Gallimard.

Duschinsky, Robbie (2014), 'Féminités schizoïdes et espaces interstitials. Enfance et genre dans *Tomboy* de Céline Sciamma et *Peter Pan* de P. J. Hogan', *Diogène* (Jan.–Mar.): 196–214.

Edney, Gemma (2020), 'Electronica, gender and French cinematic girlhood in Céline Sciamma's films', *French Screen Studies* 20.3–4: 285–97.

Emiliani, Simone (2013), 'Céline Sciamma', *Cineforum* 523: 53–4.

English, Jeri (2019), 'Childhood and gender panic in *Ma Vie en rose* and *Tomboy*', in Romain Cahreyron and Gilles Viennot (eds), *Screening Youth in Contemporary French and Francophone Cinema*, Edinburgh: Edinburgh University Press, pp. 33–46.

Felperin, Leslie (2019), '"Portrait of a Lady on Fire" ("Portrait de la jeune fille en feu"): Film review Cannes 2019', 19 May, <https://www.hollywood-reporter.com/review/portrait-a-lady-fire-review-1212091> (last accessed 11 March 2021).

Fournier, Crystel (2014), Interview at Cannes 2014 by the ARRI Channel, <https://www.youtube.com/watch?v=XqjiNyB3olw> (last accessed 11 March 2021).

Fraisse, Geneviève (2019), *La Suite de l'histoire: Actrices, créatrices*, Paris: Éditions du Seuil.

Fumaroli, Marc (2015), *'Mundus muliebris' Elisabeth Vigée Le Brun, peintre de l'Ancien régime féminin*, Paris: Éditions de Fallois.

Garbarz, Franck and Dominique Martinez (2014), 'Entretien avec Céline Sciamma: Radiographer l'étrangeté des corps', *Positif* (Oct.): 25–8.

Garcia, Manon (2018), *On ne naît pas soumise, on le devient*, Paris: Flammarion.

Gibson, Brian (2016), 'Falling for innocence: Transchild freedom vs. adult judgement in *Tomboy* and *Ma Vie en rose*', *Children's Literature* 44: 219–37.

Gilson, Nicolas (2016), 'Interview: Céline Sciamma', 2 March, <http://www.ungrandmoment.be/celine-sciamma-entrevue-2/> (last accessed 11 March 2021).

Goldin, Nan (2014), *Eden and After*, London and New York: Phaidon.

Goldin, Nan (2016), *Diving for Pearls*, Hanover: Steidl/Kestner Gesellschaft.

Halberstam, Judith (Jack) (2004), 'Oh bondage up yours! Female masculinity and the tomboy', in Steven Bruhm and Natasha Hurley (eds), *Curiouser: On the Queerness of Children*, Minneapolis, MN and London: University of Minnesota Press, pp. 191–214.

Handyside, Fiona and Kate Taylor-Jones (2015), *International Cinema and the Girl: Local Issues, Transnational Contexts*, London: Palgrave Macmillan.

Hartman, Saidiya (2019), *Wayward Lives, Beautiful Experiments*, London: Serpent's Tail.

H.D. (1982), *Collected Poems 1912–1944*, New York: New Directions.

Ince, Kate (2017), *The Body and the Screen: Female Subjectivities in Contemporary Women's Cinema*, London: Bloomsbury.

Jansen, Charlotte (2017), *Girl on Girl: Art and Photography in the Age of the Female Gaze*, London: Laurence King Publishing.

Jonet, M. Catherine (2017), 'Desire and queer adolescence: Céline Sciamma's *Naissance des Pieuvres*', *The Journal of Popular Culture* 50.5: 1127–42.

Kaganski, Serge (2014), *'Bande de filles* de Céline Sciamma', *Les Inrockuptibles*, 22 October, pp. 66–7.

Kristeva, Julia (2012), *The Severed Head: Capital Visions*, trans. Jody Gladding, New York: Columbia University Press.

Lafont, Anne (2019), 'Madeleine', in Collective, *Le Modèle noir de Géricault à Matisse*, Paris: Flammarion, pp. 58–9.

Lalanne, Jean-Marc (2007), '*Naissance des pieuvres* de Céline Sciamma', *Les Inrockuptibles*, 31 July (accessed in the Bibliothèque du film press dossier on Céline Sciamma).

Lalanne, Jean-Marc (2014), 'Bande originale', interview with Céline Sciamma, *Les Inrockuptibles*, 22 October, pp. 42–8.

Lane, Anthony (2019), 'History girls: "The Aeronauts" and "Portrait of a Lady on Fire"', *The New Yorker*, 9 December, pp. 78–9.

Lebeau, Vicky (2008), *Childhood and Cinema*, London: Reaktion.

Lindner, Katharina (2017), *Film Bodies: Queer Feminist Encounters with Gender and Sexuality in Cinema*, London: I.B. Tauris.

LMC (Le Mauvais Coton), '*Quand on a 17 ans*: Rencontre avec Céline Sciamma', 30 March, <https://www.youtube.com/watch?v=FuGquppIsm0> (last accessed 11 March 2021).

Lübecker, Nikolaj (2015), *The Feel-Bad Film*, Edinburgh: Edinburgh University Press.

Lury, Karen (2010), *The Child in Film: Tears, Fears and Fairy Tales*, London: I.B. Tauris.

McFadden, Cybelle (2014), *Gendered Frames, Embodied Cameras: Varda, Akerman, Cabrera, Calle, and Maïwenn*, Madison, NJ: Fairleigh Dickinson University Press.

McNeill, Isabelle (2018), '"Shine bright like a diamond": Music, performance and digitextuality in Céline Sciamma's *Bande de filles* (2014)', *Studies in French Cinema* 18.4: 326–40.

Madani, Ahmed (2017), Illumination(s) *suivi de* F(l)ammes, Arles: Actes Sud.

Maïga, Aïssa, Nadège Beausson-Diagne, Mata Gabib, Maïmouna Gueye, Eye Haïdara, Rachel Khan, Sara Martins, Marie-Philomène Nga, Sabine Pakora, Firmine Richard, Sonia Rolland, Magaajyia Silberfeld, Shirley Souagnon, Assa Sylla, Karidja Touré, and France Zobda (2018), *Noire n'est pas mon métier*, Paris: Éditions du Seuil.

Malabou, Catherine (2020), *Le Plaisir effacé: Clitoris et pensée*, Paris: Éditions Payot et Rivages.

Marques, Sandrine (2014), 'Place aux héroïnes de banlieue', *Le Monde*, 'Culture et idées', 18 October, p. 2.

Mathon, Claire (2019), 'Où Claire Mathon, AFC, parle de son travail sur "Portrait de la jeune fille en feu", de Céline Sciamma', <https://www.afcinema.com/Ou-Claire-Mathon-AFC-parle-de-son-travail-sur-Portrait-de-la-jeune-fille-en-feu-de-Celine-Sciamma-13478.html?lang=fr> (last accessed 11 March 2021).

Mavor, Carol (1996), *Pleasures Taken: Performances of Sexuality and Loss in Victorian Photographs*, Durham, NC: Duke University Press.

Mavor, Carol (2007), *Reading Boyishly: Roland Barthes, J. M. Barrie, Jacques Henri Lartigue, Marcel Proust, and D. W. Winnicott*, Durham, NC: Duke University Press.

Mavor, Carol (2012), *Black and Blue: The Bruising Passion of* Camera Lucida, La Jetée, Sans soleil, *and* Hiroshima mon amour, Durham, NC and London: Duke University Press.

Mavor, Carol (2013), *Blue Mythologies: Reflections on a Colour*, London: Reaktion Books.

Mayer, So (2011), *The Private Parts of Girls*, London: Salt.

Mayer, So (2015), 'She's getting back in the frame: Interview with Céline Sciamma', 5 May, <https://thefword.org.uk/2015/05/celine_sciamma_interview/> (last accessed 11 March 2021).

Mayer, So (2016), *Political Animals: The New Feminist Cinema*, London and New York: I.B. Tauris.

Meyer-Thoss, Christiane (1992), *Louise Bourgeois: Designing for Free Fall*, Zurich: Ink Press.

Miano, Léonora (2012), *Habiter la frontière*, Paris: L'Arche.

Miano, Léonora (2017), *Marianne et le garçon noir*, Paris: Pauvert.

Miano, Léonora (2020), *Afropea: utopie post-occidentale et post-raciste*, Paris: Bernard Grasset.

Mistry, Anupa (2015), '*Girlhood*: Finally, a film about black girls strengthening each other', *Jezebel*, 17 January, <http://themuse.jezebel.com/girlhood-finally-a-film-about-black-girls-strengtheni-1681462966> (last accessed 11 March 2021).

Morain, Jean-Baptiste (2019), '*Portrait de la jeune fille en feu* de Céline Sciamma', *Les Inrockuptibles*, 22 May, p. 40.

Morel, Geneviève (2012), 'Genre, surmoi et interpellation. À propos de *Tomboy* de Céline Sciamma', *Enfances & Psy* 57.4: 65–74.

Nastasi, Alison (2015), '"Girlhood" director Céline Sciamma on reclaiming childhood, casting her girl gang, and how her film mirrors "Boyhood"', FLAVORWIRE, 30 January, <http://flavorwire.com/502100/girlhood-director-celine-sciamma-on-reclaiming-childhood-casting-her-girl-gang-and-how-her-film-mirrors-boyhood> (last accessed 11 March 2021).

Niang, Mame-Fatou, Twitter thread, <https://twitter.com/mariannesnoires/status/1110368744264613893> (last accessed 11 March 2021).

Niang, Mame-Fatou (2019), *Identités françaises: Banlieues, féminisme et universalisme*, Leiden and Boston: Brill-Rodopi.

Olds, Sharon (2016), *Odes*, London: Jonathan Cape.

Ovid (1955), *Metamorphoses*, trans. with introduction by Mary M. Innes, London: Penguin.

Palmer, Tim (2011), *Brutal Intimacy: Analysing Contemporary French Cinema*, Middletown, CT: Wesleyan University Press.

Pember, Alice (2020), '"Visions of ecstasy": Resilience and melancholy in the musical moments of *Bande de filles* (Céline Sciamma, 2014)', *French Screen Studies* 20.3–4: 298–316.

Péron, Didier and Elisabeth Franck-Dumas (2014), '"Bande de filles": Une jeunesse française', *Libération*, 17 October, <http://next.liberation.fr/cinema/2014/10/17/bande-de-filles-une-jeunesse-francaise_1124323> (last accessed 11 March 2021).

Pollock, Griselda (2007), *Encounters in the Virtual Feminist Museum: Time, Space and the Archive*, London: Routledge.

Pollock, Griselda (2018), 'Action, activism, and art and/as thought: A dialogue with the artworking of Sonia Khurana and Sutapa Biswas and the political theory of Hannah Arendt', *e-flux* 92 (June), <https://www.e-flux.com/journal/92/204726/action-activism-and-art-and-as-thought-a-dialogue-with-the-artworking-of-sonia-khurana-and-sutapa-biswas-and-the-political-theory-of-hannah-arendt/> (last accessed 11 March 2021).

Preciado, Paul B. (2013), *Testo Junkie: Sex, Drugs, and Biopolitics in the Pharmacopornographic Era*, New York: The Feminist Press at the City University of New York.

Preciado, Paul B. (2019), *Un Appartement sur Uranus*, Paris: Grasset.

Preciado, Paul B. (2020a), *An Apartment on Uranus*, trans. Charlotte Mandell, London: Fitzcarraldo Editions.

Preciado, Paul B. (2020b), *Je suis un monstre qui vous parle: Rapport pour une académie de psychanalystes*, Paris: Grasset.

Proust, Marcel (1989), *À la recherche du temps perdu*, vol. 1, Paris: Gallimard.

Proust, Marcel (1996), *In Search of Lost Time*, I, *Swann's Way*, trans. C. K. Scott Moncrieff and Terence Kilmartin, rev. D. J. Enright, London: Vintage.

Regnier, Isabelle (2014), 'Amazones franches', *Le Monde*, 22 October, p. 21.

Rich, B. Ruby (2013), *New Queer Cinema*, Durham, NC and London: Duke University Press.

Romney, Jonathan (2015), 'Interview: The stars of *Girlhood*: "Our poster is all over Paris, with four black faces on it. . ."', *The Guardian*, 26 April, <https://www.theguardian.com/film/2015/apr/26/girlhood-film-karidja-toure-assa-sylla-celine-sciamma> (last accessed 11 March 2021).

Roth, Joseph (2004), *The White Cities: Reports from France 1925–39*, trans. with introduction by Michael Hofmann, London: Granta Books.

Royer, Michelle (2019), *Marguerite Duras: Multisensoriality and Female Subjectivity*, Edinburgh: Edinburgh University Press.

Saunders, Keeley (2014), 'Gender-defined spaces, places and tropes: Contemporary transgender representation in *Tomboy* and *Romeos*', *Journal of European Popular Culture* 5.2: 181–93.

Sciamma, Céline (2011a), '*Tomboy*: Director interview', on Peccadillo Pictures DVD of *Tomboy*.

Sciamma, Céline (2011b), 'Entretien', on Pyramide Vidéo DVD of *Tomboy*.

Sciamma, Céline (2011c), '*Tomboy*: Interview de Céline Sciamma and réactions des spectateurs', yaggTV, <https://www.youtube.com/watch?v=c_iNpz56hJg> (last accessed 11 March 2021).

Sciamma, Céline (2012), Interview with Joachim Lepastier, *Cahiers du cinéma* 681 (Sept.): 24–6.

Sciamma, Céline (2015), 'Director commentary', on Pyramide Distribution DVD of *Girlhood*.

Sciamma, Céline (2018), 'Céline Sciamma: Il est temps d'écrire pour soi', interview with Télérama, 26 April, <https://www.youtube.com/watch?v=yW7xjOyPJpo> (last accessed 11 March 2021).

Sciamma, Céline (2019), 'L'Égalité est le grand projet de mon travail', interview for 'She Cannes' podcast, 7 June, <https://podtail.com/fr/podcast/she-cannes/celine-sciamma-l-egalite-est-le-grand-projet-de-mo/> (last accessed 11 March 2021).

Scott, A. O. (2015), 'Exploring the limits in a man's world: In *Girlhood* a French adolescent comes out of her shell', *New York Times*, 29 January, <https://www.nytimes.com/2015/01/30/movies/in-girlhood-a-french-adolescent-comes-out-of-her-shell.html?_r=0> (last accessed 11 March 2021).

Sellier, Geneviève (2005), *Masculine Singular: French New Wave Cinema*, trans. Kristin Ross, Durham, NC: Duke University Press.

Sharpe, Christina (2016), *In the Wake: On Blackness and Being*, Durham, NC and London: Duke University Press.

Smith, Frances (2020), Bande de filles: *Girlhood Identities in Contemporary France*, London: Routledge.

Sotinel, Thomas (2019), 'Tableau d'une révolution amoureuse', *Le Monde*, 18 September, p. 25.

Soumahoro, Maboula (2020), *Le Triangle et l'hexagone: Réflexions sur une identité noire*, Paris: La Découverte.

Springora, Vanessa (2020), *Le Consentement*, Paris: Grasset.

Stockton, Kathryn Bond (2009), *The Queer Child, or Growing Sideways in the Twentieth Century*, Durham, NC and London: Duke University Press.

Tessé, Jean-Philippe (2019), 'Portrait de la jeune fille en feu de Céline Sciamma', *Cahiers du cinéma* 758 (Sept.): 43.

Vergès, Françoise (2019), *Un féminisme décolonial*, Paris: La Fabrique.

Vigée Le Brun, Elisabeth [1842] (2015), *Souvenirs*, Paris: Champion.

Vincendeau, Ginette (2015), 'Minority report', *Sight and Sound* (June): 25–31.

Waldron, Darren (2013), 'Embodying gender nonconformity in "Girls": Céline Sciamma's *Tomboy*', *L'Esprit créateur* 53.1: 60–73.

Wheatley, Catherine (2011), '*Tomboy*', *Sight and Sound* 21.10: 79–80.

Wilson, Emma (2012a), 'Beauvoir's children: Girlhood in *Innocence*', in Jean-Pierre Boulé and Ursula Tidd (eds), *Existentialism and Contemporary Cinema*, New York and London: Berghahn Books, pp. 17–31.

Wilson, Emma (2012b), 'Precarious lives: On girls in Mia Hansen-Løve and others', *Studies in French Cinema* 12.3: 273–84.

Wilson, Emma (2014), '"The sea nymphs tested this miracle": *Water Lilies* (2007) and the origin of coral', in Chris Brown and Pam Hirsch (eds), *The Cinema of the Swimming Pool*, Oxford, Bern, Berlin, Brussels, Frankfurt am Main, New York, and Vienna: Peter Lang, pp. 203–14.

Wilson, Emma (2017), 'Scenes of hurt and rapture: Céline Sciamma's *Girlhood*', *Film Quarterly* 70.3: 10–22.

Wilson, Emma (2019), *The Reclining Nude: Agnès Varda, Catherine Breillat, and Nan Goldin*, Liverpool: Liverpool University Press.

Wilson, Emma (2021), 'Maternal eroticism: Queering Isabelle Huppert', in Nick Rees-Roberts and Darren Waldron (eds), *Isabelle Huppert: Stardom, Performance, Authorship*, New York: Bloomsbury, pp. 99–115.

Wood, Jason (2014), *Last Words: Considering Contemporary Cinema*, New York: Columbia University Press.

Filmography

Sciamma as director

Naissance des pieuvres [*Water Lilies*] (2007)
Screenplay: Céline Sciamma
Producers: Bénédicte Couvreur and Jérôme Dopffer
Music: Jean-Baptiste de Laubier (as Para One)
Cinematography: Crystel Fournier
Editor: Julien Lacheray
Marie: Pauline Acquart
Anne: Louise Blachère
Floriane: Adèle Haenel

Pauline (2010)
Screenplay: Daphné Charbonneau
Cinematography: Julien Poupard
Editor: Julien Lacheray
Pauline: Anaïs Demoustier
Girlfriend: Adèle Haenel

Tomboy (2011)
Screenplay: Céline Sciamma
Producers: Rémi Burah, Bénédicte Couvreur, and Tiphaine Perin
Music: Jean-Baptiste de Laubier (as Para One) and Jérôme Echenoz
Cinematography: Crystel Fournier
Editor: Julien Lacheray
Laure/Mickäel: Zoé Héran
Jeanne: Malonn Lévana
Lisa: Jeanne Disson
La mère: Sophie Cattani
Le père: Mathieu Demy

Bande de filles [*Girlhood*] (2014)
Screenplay: Céline Sciamma
Producers: Rémi Burah, Bénédicte Couvreur, and Olivier Père
Music: Jean-Baptiste de Laubier (as Para One)
Cinematography: Crystel Fournier
Editor: Julien Lacheray
Marieme/Vic: Karidja Touré
Lady: Assa Sylla
Adiatou: Lindsay Karamoh
Fily: Mariétou Touré
Ismaël: Idrissa Diabaté
Bébé: Simina Soumaré
Monica: Dielika Coulibaly
Djibril: Cyril Mendy
Abou: Djibril Gueye
Asma: Binta Diop
Mini: Chance N'Guessan

Portrait de la jeune fille en feu [*Portrait of a Lady on Fire*] (2019)
Screenplay: Céline Sciamma
Producers: Rémi Burah, Véronique Cayla, Bénédicte Couvreur, and Olivier Père
Music: Jean-Baptiste de Laubier and Arthus Simonini
Cinematography: Claire Mathon
Editor: Julien Lacheray
Marianne: Noémie Merlant
Héloïse: Adèle Haenel
Sophie: Luàna Bajrami
La Comtesse: Valeria Golino

Other films

Les Rendez-vous d'Anna [*The Meetings of Anna*] (Chantal Akerman, 1978)
Portrait d'une jeune fille de la fin des années 60 à Bruxelles [*Portrait of a Young Girl in the Late 60s in Brussels*] (Chantal Akerman, 1994)
Mysterious Skin (Gregg Araki, 2004)
Les Olympiades (Jacques Audiard, 2021)
Ma Vie de Courgette [*My Life as a Courgette*] (Claude Barras, 2016)
Divines (Houda Benyamina, 2016)
Viskningar och rop [*Cries and Whispers*] (Ingmar Bergman, 1972)
Ma Vie en rose (Alain Berliner, 1997)

La Cour de Babel [*School of Babel*] (Julie Bertuccelli, 2013)
Une Vraie Jeune Fille [*A Real Young Girl*] (Catherine Breillat, 1976)
Romance (Catherine Breillat, 1999)
Les Estivants [*The Summer House*] (Valeria Bruni Tedeschi, 2018)
A Girl's Own Story (Jane Campion, 1986)
The Piano (Jane Campion, 1993)
The Portrait of a Lady (Jane Campion, 1996)
In the Cut (Jane Campion, 2003)
Entre les murs [*The Class*] (Laurent Cantet, 2008)
La Belle Saison [*Summertime*] (Catherine Corsini, 2015)
Les Demoiselles de Rochefort (Jacques Demy, 1967)
35 rhums [*35 Shots of Rum*] (Claire Denis, 2008)
Girl (Lukas Dhont, 2018)
La Mort de Danton (Alice Diop, 2011)
La Permanence (Alice Diop, 2016)
Vers la tendresse [*Towards Tenderness*] (Alice Diop, 2016)
Atlantique [*Atlantics*] (Mati Diop, 2019)
Ponette (Jacques Doillon, 1996)
Mignonnes [*Cuties*] (Maïmouna Doucouré, 2020)
Grave [*Raw*] (Julia Ducournau, 2016)
Mina Tannenbaum (Martine Dugowson, 1994)
Le Daim [*Deerskin*] (Quentin Dupieux, 2019)
Ouvrir la voix [*Speak Up*] (Amandine Gay, 2017)
L'Inconnu du lac [*Stranger by the Lake*] (Alain Guiraudie, 2013)
The Souvenir (Joanna Hogg, 2019)
La Haine (Mathieu Kassovitz, 1995)
Kokon [*Cocoon*] (Leonie Krippendorf, 2020)
Petite fille [*Little Girl*] (Sébastien Lifshitz, 2020)
La Vie ne me fait pas peur [*Life Doesn't Scare Me*] (Noémie Lvovsky, 1999)
Mulholland Drive (David Lynch, 2001)
Polisse (Maïwenn, 2011)
Le Souffle au coeur [*Murmur of the Heart*] (Louis Malle, 1971)
L'Heure de la sortie [*School's Out*] (Sébastien Marnier, 2018)
The Holy Girl (Lucrecia Martel, 2004)
Lola vers la mer [*Lola*] (Laurent Mikeli, 2019)
L'Effrontée [*An Impudent Girl*] (Claude Miller, 1985)
La Petite Voleuse [*The Little Thief*] (Claude Miller, 1988)
Lilya 4-ever (Lukas Moodysson, 2002)
Mariannes noires (Mame-Fatou Niang and Kaytie Nielsen, 2016)
Teorema [*Theorem*] (Pier Paolo Pasolini, 1968)
Boys Don't Cry (Kimberly Peirce, 1999)
La Boum [*The Party*] (Claude Pinoteau, 1980)

Leaving Neverland: Michael Jackson and Me (Dan Reed, 2019)

L'Ami de mon amie [*My Girlfriend's Boyfriend*] (Eric Rohmer, 1987)

En Liberté [*The Trouble with You*] (Pierre Salvadori, 2018)

Nous, princesses de Clèves [*Children of the Princess of Cleves*] (Régis Sauder, 2011)

Les Témoins [*The Witnesses*] (André Téchiné, 2007)

Quand on a 17 ans [*Being 17*] (André Téchiné, 2016)

Les 400 coups [*Four Hundred Blows*] (François Truffaut, 1959)

Nan Goldin, In My Life (Paul Tschinkel, 1997, ART/new york, No. 47. A video series on contemporary art)

L'Une chante, l'autre pas [*One Sings, the Other Doesn't*] (Agnès Varda, 1977)

Documenteur (Agnès Varda, 1981)

Jane B. par Agnès V. [*Jane B. by Agnès V.*] (Agnès Varda, 1988)

Une Fille facile [*An Easy Girl*] (Rebecca Zlotowski, 2019)

Index